W9-AWN-577

THE
FOURTEEN
HOLY HELPERS

St. Blaise saves a child from choking to death on a fishbone.

THE
FOURTEEN
HOLY HELPERS

EARLY CHRISTIAN SAINTS
WHO ARE POWERFUL WITH GOD

INCLUDING NOVENA PRAYERS

Compiled by

Fr. Bonaventure Hammer, O.F.M.

*"And the smoke of the incense of the prayers
of the saints ascended up before God from the
hand of the angel."*
—Apocalypse 8:4

TAN BOOKS AND PUBLISHERS, INC.
Rockford, Illinois 61105

Imprimi Permittitur: Fr. Chrysostomus Theobald, O.F.M.
                               Minister Provincialis
                               Cincinnati, Ohio
                               March 30, 1908

Nihil Obstat: Remy Lafort, S.T.L.
                               Censor Librorum

Imprimatur: ✠ John M. Farley
                               Archbishop of New York
                               New York
                               March 4, 1909

"God is wonderful in his saints: the God of Israel is he who will give power and strength to his people. Blessed be God."

—*Psalm* 67:36

Contents

NOVENA TO ALL THE HOLY HELPERS

Prayers and Petitions

Preface

THE contents of the following pages are based on the Catholic doctrine of the veneration and invocation of the saints, and of the efficacy of the prayer of intercession. The legends of the individual "Holy Helpers" were compiled from authors whose writings have the approval of the Church.

In compliance with the decrees of Pope Urban VIII of 1625, 1631, and 1634, the compiler formally declares that he submits everything contained in this little book to the infallible judgment of the Church, and that he claims no other than human credibility for the facts, legends, and miracles related, except where the Church has otherwise decided.

THE COMPILER.

THE
FOURTEEN
HOLY HELPERS

PART I

The Fourteen Holy Helpers

"The souls of the just are in the hand of God, and the torment of death shall not touch them. In the sight of the unwise they seemed to die, and their departure was taken for misery, and their going away from us for utter destruction; but they are in peace. And though in the sight of men they suffered torments, their hope is full of immortality. Afflicted in few things, in many they shall be well rewarded; because God hath tried them, and found them worthy of Himself" (*Wis.* iii. 1-5.)

CHAPTER I

The Fourteen Holy Helpers

AMONG the saints who in Catholic devotion are invoked with special confidence, because they have proved themselves efficacious helpers in adversity and difficulties, there is a group venerated under the collective name of Holy Helpers. They are:

1. St. George, Martyr.
2. St. Blase, Bishop and Martyr.
3. St. Pantaleon, Martyr.
4. St. Vitus, Martyr.
5. St. Erasmus, Bishop and Martyr.
6. St. Christophorus, Martyr.
7. St. Dionysius, Bishop and Martyr.
8. St. Cyriacus, Martyr.
9. St. Achatius, Martyr.
10. St. Eustachius, Martyr.
11. St. Giles, Abbot.
12. St. Catherine, Virgin and Martyr.
13. St. Margaret, Virgin and Martyr.
14. St. Barbara, Virgin and Martyr.

The reason why these saints are invoked as a group is said to have been an epidemic which devastated Europe from 1346 to 1349. It was called

---

Note: St. Erasmus is also called St. Elmo; St. Christophorus is usually called St. Christopher; St. Dionysius is also known as St. Denis; St. Cyriacus is also called St. Cyriac; and St. Eustachius is also called St. Eustace. Traditional feast day of the 14 Holy Helpers: August 8.

the Plague, or "Black Death," and among its symptoms were the turning black of the tongue, parching of the throat, violent headache, fever, and boils on the abdomen. The malady attacked its victims suddenly, bereft them of reason, and caused death in a few hours, so that many died without the last sacraments. Fear caused many attacks and disrupted social and family ties. To all appearances, the disease was incurable.

During this period of general affliction the people in pious confidence turned toward Heaven, and had recourse to the intercession of the saints, praying to be spared an attack, or to be cured when stricken. Among the saints invoked since the earliest times of the Church as special patrons in certain diseases were: St. Christopher and St. Giles against the plague, St. Dionysius against headache, St. Blase against ills of the throat, St. Catherine against those of the tongue, St. Erasmus against those of the abdomen, St. Barbara against fever, St. Vitus against epilepsy. St. Pantaleon was the patron of physicians, St. Cyriacus was had recourse to in temptations, especially in those at the hour of death; St. Achatius was invoked in death agony; Sts. Christopher, Barbara, and Catherine were appealed to for protection against a sudden and unprovided death; the aid of St. Giles was implored for

---

Note: See the individual chapters on these saints for additional information on their patronage.

making a good confession; St. Eustachius was patron in all kinds of difficulties, and, because peculiar circumstances separated him for a time from his family, he was invoked also in family troubles. Domestic animals, too, being attacked by the plague, Sts. George, Erasmus, Pantaleon, and Vitus were invoked for their protection. It appears from the invocation of these saints, so widespread in olden times during the plague and other epidemics, that their being grouped as the Fourteen Holy Helpers originated in a like visitation.

The fourteen saints venerated as the Holy Helpers are represented with the symbols of their martyrdom, or with the insignia of their state of life; also, as a group of children. The latter representation is accounted for as follows:

The abbey of Langheim, in the diocese of Bamberg, Bavaria, owned a farm on which the monks kept their flocks. The sheep were tended by shepherds, who led them along the hillsides, where they grazed quietly during the day, and were driven home in the evening.

On the evening of September 22, 1445, a young shepherd, Herman Leicht, who was gathering his flock for the homeward drive, heard what seemed to him to be the cry of a child, and looking about, saw a child sitting in a field near by. Surprised, and wondering how the child came there, he was about to approach, when it disappeared. Feeling rather disturbed, the boy returned to his flock. After reaching it, he turned to look back to the place where he had seen the apparition. There the child sat again, this time in a circle of light, and between two burning candles. Terrified at this second apparition, he made the sign of the cross. The child smiled, as if to encourage him, and he was about to approach it again, when it vanished a second time. Greatly perplexed, he drove his flock home and informed his parents of the occurrence. But they called the apparition a delusion and told him not to mention it to any one. Nevertheless, feeling uneasy, and desiring an explanation, he went to the monastery and related his experience to one of the Fathers, who advised him to ask the child, if it ever should appear to him again, what it wanted.

Nearly a year later, June 28, 1446, the eve of the feast of Sts. Peter and Paul, the child again appeared to the boy in the same place as before and about sunset; but this time it was surrounded by thirteen other children, all in a halo of glory. He boldly approached the group and asked the child he had formerly seen in the name of the Father, and of the Son, and the Holy Ghost, what it desired. The child replied: "We are the Fourteen Helpers, and desire that a chapel be built for us. Be thou our servant, and we shall serve thee." Then the group of children disappeared, and the shepherd boy was filled with heavenly consolation.

The following Sunday, after he had driven his flock to the pasture, it seemed to him that he saw two lighted candles descending from the sky to the place where he had seen the apparition. A woman who was passing at the time declared that she also saw them. The boy hastened to the monastery and told about the two apparitions. The abbot, Frederic IV, and the rest of the community, were not inclined to believe in the apparition, and ascribed it to the boy's visionary fancy. But when, in the course of time, several extraordinary favors were granted to people who prayed at the place of the apparition, the monks built a chapel there. It was begun in 1447, and finished and dedicated next year under the invocation of the Blessed Virgin Mary and the Fourteen Holy Helpers. The bishop granted an indulgence for the day of the anniversary of the dedication, the Papal Nuncio, Cardinal Joannes, granted another, and Pope Nicholas V a third. These indulgences, and a number of other spiritual privileges granted to the chapel, attracted a great many visitors, so that it became a place of pious pilgrimage. Elector Frederic III, in fulfilment of a vow made when beset with difficulties, visited the chapel in 1485. Emperor Ferdinand also visited it and left, as a votive offering, his gold pectoral chain on the altar.

Devotion to the Fourteen Holy Helpers continued to spread. In 1743, a magnificent church, to replace the old chapel, was begun, and completed in 1772. Churches and altars in honor of these saints are found in Italy, Austria, Tyrol, Hungary, Bohemia, Switzerland, and other countries of Europe. In the United States of America two churches are dedicated under the invocation of the Holy Helpers: one in Baltimore, Md., the other in Gardenville, N. Y. Wherever and whenever invoked, these saints have proved themselves willing helpers in all difficulties, vicissitudes, and trials of their faithful clients.

CHAPTER II

Legends

BEFORE proceeding to relate the lives of the Fourteen Holy Helpers, we deem it opportune to define the term usually applied to the narrative of the lives of the saints.

The histories of the saints are called Legends. This word is derived from the Latin, and signifies something that is to be read, a passage the reading of which is prescribed. The legends of the saints are the lives of the holy martyrs and confessors of the Faith. Some of them occur in the Roman Breviary which the Catholic clergy is obliged to read every day.

Joseph von Goerres, an illustrious champion of the Church during the first half of the nineteenth century, writes as follows concerning legends:

"The histories of the lives of the saints were gathered from the earliest times. A collection of such histories is found in 'The Golden Legend.' The Passionales, too, containing the life of a saint for every day in the year, belong to this sort of literature. In Germany these histories were at first translations from the Latin; later, they were written in the native idiom, and, in style, were of a charming simplicity. At that time, when the upper classes did not yet judge themselves too highly cultivated to share in the Faith, and not too privileged to join in the sentiments and affections of the people, and were therefore more in harmony with the lower ranks of society, these legends were in general circulation among all classes: among the wealthy in manuscript, among the poor orally and in the form in which they had become acquainted with them in church and elsewhere.

"In early times the science of criticism was unknown; therefore little care was exercised in separating the poetic additions from the authentic legends, especially as the Church had not yet spoken on the subject. Faith was yet of that robust sort which is not affected by miraculous occurrences. Nearly all Europe then still accepted the adage now current only in Spain, 'It is better sometimes to believe what can not be established as truth, than to lose a single truth by want of faith.' But later the science of criticism came into its rights. The Church established canonical rules, according to which a strict investigation of all the facts submitted to her judgment was to be made, and rejected everything that could not stand the most rigid examination.

"Then Art devoted itself to that legendary lore

which the Church, declaring it outside of her domain, permitted to be embellished at will. Thus poetic legends were multiplied, their authors being more or less convinced that the reader would be able to distinguish truth from poetical embellishment. The common people continued to make little distinction and did not permit criticism to influence their ancient beliefs. They regarded these legends as they regard the pictures of the saints; not as portraits of the persons depicted—for in the very next church the same saint might be represented in a quite different manner—but as illustrations, more or less apt, whose object was to attract the attention by their artistic character and thus to draw the mind to the contemplation of their original, and by it to God, and thereby serve the purpose of edification."

If we are not devoid of all sentiments of piety, the history of the combats and victories of the saints and martyrs, and the narrative of the miracles wrought through their intercession before and after their death, will always be a source of joy and consolation to us, and will tend to animate us with similar fortitude and love of virtue.

The legends of the Fourteen Holy Helpers are replete with the most glorious examples of heroic firmness and invincible courage in the profession of the Faith, which ought to incite us to imitate their fidelity in the performance of the Christian and social duties. If they, with the aid of God's grace, achieved such victories, why should not we, by the same aid, be able to accomplish the little desired of us? God rewarded His victorious champions with eternal bliss; the same crown is prepared for us, if we but render ourselves worthy of it. God placed the seal of miracles on the intrepid confession of His servants; and a mind imbued with the spirit of faith sees nothing extraordinary therein, because our divine Saviour Himself said, "Amen, amen I say to you, he that believeth in Me, the works that I do, he also shall do, and greater than these shall he do" (*John* xiv. 12). In all the miraculous events wrought in and by the saints appears only the victorious omnipotent power of Jesus Christ, and the living faith in which His servants operated in virtue of this power. To obliterate the miracles that appear in the lives of the saints, or even to enfeeble their import by the manner of relating them, would rob these legends of their intrinsic value. If our age is no longer robust enough to acknowledge the effects of divine omnipotence and grace, it does not follow that they must be disavowed or denied.

I

St. George, Martyr

LEGEND

ST. GEORGE is honored throughout Christendom as one of the most illustrious martyrs of Jesus Christ. In the reign of the first Christian emperors numerous churches were erected in his honor, and his tomb in Palestine became a celebrated place of pilgrimage. But his history is involved in great obscurity, as no early records of his life and martyrdom are at present in existence. The following are the traditions concerning him which have been handed down to us by the Greek historians, and which are celebrated in verse by that illustrious saint and poet of the eighth century, St. John Damascene.

St. George is said to have been born in Cappadocia of noble Christian parents. After the death of his father, he traveled with his mother into Palestine, of which she was a native. There she possessed a considerable estate, which fell to him upon her death. Being strong and robust in body, he embraced the profession of a soldier, and was made a tribune, or colonel, in the army. His courage and fidelity attracted the attention of

Note: St. George is a patron of soldiers, as well as patron of England, Portugal, Germany, Aragon, Genoa and Venice. St. George is invoked in herpetic diseases. Traditional feast day: April 23.

Emperor Diocletian, who bestowed upon him marks of special favor. When that prince declared war against the Christian religion, St. George laid aside the signs of his rank, threw up his commission, and rebuked the emperor for the severity of his bloody edicts. He was immediately cast into prison, and alternate threats and promises were employed to induce him to apostatize. As he continued firm, he was put to the torture and tormented with great cruelty. "I despise your promises," he said to the judge, "and do not fear your threats. The emperor's power is of short duration, and his reign will soon end. It were better for you, to acknowledge the true God and to seek His kingdom." Thereupon a great block of stone was placed on the breast of the brave young officer, and thus he was left in prison.

Next day he was bound upon a wheel set with sharp knives, and it was put in motion to cut him to pieces. Whilst suffering this cruel torture, he saw a heavenly vision, which consoled and encouraged him, saying, "George, fear not; I am with thee." His patience and fortitude under the torments inflicted on him so affected the numerous pagan spectators that many of them were converted to the Faith and suffered martyrdom for it. On the next day, April 23, 303, St. George was led through the city and beheaded. This took place at Lydda, the city in which, as we read in the Acts of the Apostles (ix.), St. Peter healed a man sick with the palsy.

St. George is usually represented as a knight tilting against a dragon; but this is only emblematical of the glorious combat in which he encountered and overthrew the devil, winning for himself thereby a martyr's crown.

LESSON

W̶E̶, TOO, like St. George, often have opportunity to confess our faith in Christ. We confess it by patiently bearing adversity, by suppressing our evil inclinations, by suffering injustice without retaliating evil for evil, by using every opportunity of performing deeds of charity, by devoting ourselves unremittingly to our daily duties, by carefully guarding our tongue, etc. Examine yourself whether you have not often denied your Faith, if not in words, through your works.

Prayer of the Church

O GOD, who dost rejoice us by the merits and intercession of Thy blessed martyr George; graciously grant that we, who through him implore Thee for Thy bounty, may receive thereby the gift of Thy grace. Through Christ our Lord. Amen.

St. Blase, Bishop and Martyr

LEGEND

ST. BLASE was born at Sebaste, Armenia. He became a physician, but at the same time devoted himself zealously to the practice of his Christian duties. His virtuous conduct gained for him the esteem of the Christian clergy and people to such a degree, that he was elected bishop of his native city. Henceforth he devoted himself to ward off the dangers of soul from the faithful, as he had hitherto been intent on healing their bodily ills. To all, he was a shining example of virtue.

During the reign of Emperor Licinius a cruel persecution of Christians broke out. The persecutors directed their fury principally against the bishops, well knowing that when the shepherd is stricken the flock is dispersed. Listening to the entreaties of the faithful, and mindful of the words of Our Lord, "When they shall persecute you in this city, flee into another" (*Matt.* x. 23), St. Blase hid himself in a cave. But one day the prefect Agricola instituted a chase, and his party discovered the holy bishop and brought him before their master.

St. Blase remained steadfast in the Faith, and

Note: St. Blase's name is also spelled Blaise and Blasius. He is invoked in throat ailments. The blessing of throats takes place on his feast day, February 3 (February 11 in the Eastern Churches).

by its able confession and defense attracted the attention of the attendants at his trial. The cruel tyrant had him bound and tortured with iron combs. After suffering these torments with great patience and meekness, the saint was cast into prison. He was kept there a long time, because the prefect hoped to exhaust his powers of endurance, and to bring him to sacrifice to the idols. His jailer permitted the holy bishop to receive visitors in his prison, and many sick and suffering availed themselves of this privilege. He cured some of them and gave good advice to others.

One day a mother brought to him her boy, who, while eating, had swallowed a fishbone, which remained in his throat, and, causing great pain, threatened suffocation. St. Blase prayed and made the sign of the cross over the boy, and behold, he was cured. For this reason the saint is invoked in throat troubles.

At length the holy bishop was again brought before the judge and commanded to sacrifice to the idols. But he said: "Thou art blind, because thou art not illuminated by the true light. How can a man sacrifice to idols, when he adores the true God alone? I do not fear thy threats. Do with me according to thy pleasure. My body is in thy power, but God alone has power over my soul. Thou seekest salvation with the idols; I hope and trust to receive it from the only true and living God whom I adore."

Then the prefect sentenced him to death. St. Blase was beheaded, suffering death for the Faith February 3, 316.

LESSON

S⊤. Blase gave us a glorious example of fortitude in the confession of the Faith. According to the teaching of St. Paul, confession of the Faith is necessary for our salvation. He says, "For if thou confess with thy mouth the Lord Jesus, and believe in thy heart that God hath raised Him up from the dead, thou shalt be saved. For with the heart we believe unto justice, but with the mouth confession is made unto salvation" (*Rom.* x. 9, 10). We are, therefore, not permitted to be silent, much less to agree, when our Faith, and whatever is connected therewith, as the sacraments, ceremonies, priests, etc., are ridiculed and reviled. Parents especially must be most careful in speaking of these subjects before their children and servants, and do so only with due reverence.

On the contrary, we must confess our Faith, and if necessary, defend it against all attacks. Often one serious word will suffice to silence a calumniator of the Faith and cause him to blush. We must confess our Faith not only in the bosom of our family, but also in public. We must let our fellow-men know that we are true Catholics, who adhere to our Faith from conviction, without regard to what others say of us, or how they judge us, remembering the words of Our Lord, "Every one, therefore, that shall confess me before men, I will also confess him before my Father who is in heaven" (*Matt.* x. 32).

It was remarked above that St. Blase is the patron invoked in throat troubles. Therefore the Church, on his feast, February 3, gives a special blessing, at which she prays over those receiving it: "By the intercession of St. Blase, bishop and martyr, may God deliver thee from all ills of the throat and from all other ills; in the name of the Father, and of the Son, and of the Holy Ghost. Amen." Do not neglect to receive this blessing, if you have the opportunity. The blessings of the Church are powerful and effective, for she is God's representative on earth. Therefore her blessing is God's blessing, and is always effective, except we ourselves place an obstacle in its way.

Prayer of the Church

O GOD, who dost rejoice us through the memory of Thy blessed bishop and martyr Blase: graciously grant us, that we, who honor his memory, may experience his protection. Through Christ our Lord. Amen.

III

LEGEND

𝕿HE pious historians of the early Christian times state, as a rule, only what the saints did and suffered for the Faith, and how they died. They deemed the martyrs' glorious combat and their victorious entrance into heaven more instructive, and therefore more important, than a lengthy description of their lives.

Hence we know little of the native place and the youth of St. Erasmus, except that at the beginning of the fourth century of the Christian era he was bishop of Antioch in Asia Minor, the city where the name of "Christian" first came into use. When a long and cruel persecution broke out under the Emperor Diocletian, St. Erasmus hid himself in the mountains of the Libanon, and led there, for some years, an austere life of penance and fasting. Finally he was discovered and dragged before the judge.

At first, persuasions and kindness were employed to induce him to deny the Faith, but when these efforts failed recourse was had to the most cruel torments. He was scourged, and finally cast into a caldron filled with boiling oil, sulphur, and pitch. In this seething mass God preserved him from harm, and by this miracle many spec-

---

Note: St. Erasmus is also known as St. Elmo. He is pictured with his entrails wound around a windlass, indicating one of the tortures he suffered. St. Erasmus is invoked in stomach and intestinal disorders; he is patron of sailors. Traditional feast day: June 2.

tators were converted to the Faith. Still more enraged thereat, the judge ordered the holy bishop to be thrown into prison and kept there in chains till he died of starvation. But God delivered him, as He had once delivered St. Peter. One night an angel appeared to him and said: "Erasmus, follow me! Thou shalt convert a great many." Thus far he had led numbers to the Faith by suffering, now he was to convert multitudes as a missionary.

Delivered from prison by the power of God, he went forth into many lands and preached the Faith. Mighty in word and deed, he wrought many miracles and converted great numbers of heathens. At length he came to Italy, where Emperor Maximin persecuted the Christians as fiercely as did Diocletian in the East. As soon as Maximin heard of Erasmus and the conversions effected by his preaching and miracles, he ordered the slaughter of three hundred of the converts. Erasmus himself was most cruelly tortured, but to no purpose. He remained firm. Then cast into prison, he was again liberated by an angel.

At last the hour of deliverance came to this valiant and apostolic confessor and martyr of Christ. He heard a heavenly voice, saying: "Erasmus, come now to the heavenly city and rest in the place which God has prepared for thee with the holy martyrs and prophets. Enjoy now the fruit of thy labor. By thee I was honored in heaven and on earth." Erasmus, looking toward heaven, saw a splendid crown, and the apostles and prophets welcoming him. He bowed his head, saying: "Receive, O Lord, the soul of thy servant!" and peacefully breathed forth his spirit on June 2, 308.

LESSON

THE tortures which St. Erasmus suffered for the Faith seem almost incredible, and the events related of him are truly wonderful. Martyrdom and miracles illustrated the doctrine he preached; he converted multitudes and gained the crown of heaven.

Perhaps you say that in our times there are no longer any martyrs, at least not in civilized countries. Are you quite sure of it? St. Augustine writes: "Peace also has its martyrs." It is certainly not easy to suffer torments like the martyrs and to receive finally the death-dealing blow of the sword. But is it not also a martyrdom to suffer for years the pains of a lingering illness? Again, how difficult the combat with the world, the flesh, and the powers of hell! How carefully must we watch and pray to gain the victory! This is *our* martyrdom. Let us imitate the example of the holy martyrs in bearing the trials and sufferings of life, and we shall receive, as they did, the crown of heaven.

Prayer of the Church

O GOD, who dost give us joy through the memory of Thy holy martyrs, graciously grant that we may be inflamed by their example, in whose merits we rejoice. Through Christ our Lord. Amen.

IV

St. Pantaleon, Physician and Martyr

LEGEND

ST. PANTALEON was physician to Emperor Maximin and a Christian, but he fell through a temptation which is sometimes more dangerous than the most severe trials by the fiercest torments. This temptation was the bad example of the impious, idolatrous courtiers with whom the young physician associated. He was seduced by them and abandoned the Faith. But the grace of God called him, and he obeyed.

Hermolaus, a zealous priest, by prudent exhortation awakened Pantaleon's conscience to a sense of his guilt, and brought him back into the fold of the Church. Henceforth he devoted himself ardently to the advancement of the spiritual and temporal welfare of his fellow-citizens. First of all he sought to convert his father, who was still

Note: In the Middle Ages, St. Pantaleon was regarded as patron of physicians and midwives; he is also invoked for consumptive diseases. A vial of his blood at Constantinople is said to liquefy on his feast. Traditional feast day: July 27; also July 28 and Feb. 18.

a heathen, and had the consolation to see him die a Christian. He divided the ample fortune which he inherited amongst the poor and the sick. As a physician, he was intent on healing his patients both by physical and by spiritual means. Christians he confirmed in the practice and confession of the Faith, and the heathens he sought to convert. Many suffering from incurable diseases were restored to health by his prayer and the invocation of the holy name of Jesus. His presence was everywhere fraught with blessings and consolation.

St. Pantaleon yearned to prove his fidelity to the Faith by shedding his blood for it, and the opportunity came to him when his heathen associates in the healing art denounced him to the emperor as a zealous propagator of Christianity. He was brought up before the emperor's tribunal and ordered to sacrifice to the idols. He replied: "The God whom I adore is Jesus Christ. He created heaven and earth, He raised the dead to life, made the blind see and healed the sick, all through the power of His word. Your idols are dead, they can not do anything. Order a sick person to be brought here, one declared incurable. Your priests shall invoke their idols for him and I shall call on the only true God, and we shall see who is able to help him." The proposal was accepted. A man sick with the palsy was brought, who could neither walk nor stand without help. The heathen priests prayed for him, but in vain. Then Pantaleon prayed, took the sick man by the hand, and said: "In the name of Jesus, the Son of God, I command thee to rise and be well." And the palsied man rose, restored to perfect health.

By this miracle a great number of those present were converted. But the emperor and the idolatrous priests were all the more enraged. Maximin now attempted to gain Pantaleon by blandishments and promises to deny the Faith, but without success. Then he had recourse to threats, and as they too availed nothing, he proceeded to have them put into execution. The brave confessor of the Faith was tortured in every conceivable manner. Finally he was nailed to a tree, and then beheaded. The priest Hermolaus and the brothers Hermippos and Hermocrates suffered death with him, in the year 308.

LESSON

ℏ APPY are they who, whatever may be their station or calling in life, are intent on bringing those with whom they come into contact under the influence of religion. But, alas, too many do just the reverse. They permit themselves to be led astray by bad example, and set aside the claims of the Church as too severe and exacting. How do you act in this regard? Do you shun the company of the wicked? A proverb says: "Tell me in whose company you are found, and I will tell you who you are." Bad company insensibly undermines faith and morals, overcomes the fear of evil and the aversion to it and weakens the will. "He that loveth danger shall perish in it" (*Ecclus.* iii. 27).

As soon as St. Pantaleon came to a sense of his apostasy, he repented and returned to the practice of the Faith. He did this despite the knowledge that he thereby incurred hatred and persecution. The true Christian will ever follow the dictates of conscience and please God, whether he thereby incur the displeasure of men or not. If, to please men, we become remiss in the service of God, we show that we fear and love Him less than men. What a lamentable folly! Of whom have we to expect greater benefits or to fear greater evils—from God or man? Do not act thus unwisely; rather imitate St. Pantaleon, and live for God and His service.

Prayer of the Church

ALMIGHTY God, grant us through the intercession of Thy blessed martyr Pantaleon to be delivered and preserved from all ills of the body, and from evil thoughts and influences in spirit. Through Christ our Lord. Amen,

V

LEGEND

St. Vitus belonged to a noble pagan family of Sicily, and was born about the year 291, at Mazurra. His father, Hylas, placed him in early childhood in charge of a Christian couple named Modestus and Crescentia, who raised him in the Christian faith, and had him baptized. He grew in years and in virtue, till, at the age of twelve, he was claimed by his father, who, to his great anger, found him a fervent Christian. Convinced, after many unsuccessful attempts, that stripes and other chastisements would not induce him to renounce the Faith, his father delivered the brave boy up to Valerian, the governor, who in vain employed every artifice to shake his constancy. Finally he commanded Vitus to be scourged, but when two soldiers were about to execute this order their hands and those of Valerian were suddenly lamed. The governor ascribed this to sorcery, yet he invoked Vitus' help, and behold, when the Christian boy made the sign of the cross over the lamed members, they were healed. Then Valerian sent him back to his father, telling him to leave no means untried to induce his son to sacrifice to the idols.

Hylas now tried blandishments, pleasures, and

Note: St. Vitus (he is sometimes called St. Guy) is invoked in epilepsy, chorea ("St. Vitus Dance"), lethargy, bites of mad or poisonous animals, and storms; he is a patron of dancers and actors. Traditional feast day: June 15.

amusements to influence the brave boy. He even sent a corrupt woman to tempt him, and for that purpose locked them both together in one room. But Vitus, who had remained firm amid tortures, resisted also the allurements of sensuality. Closing his eyes, he knelt in prayer, and behold, an angel appeared, filling the room with heavenly splendor, and stood at the youth's side. Terrified, the woman fled. But even this miracle did not change the obstinate father.

Finally Vitus escaped, and with Modestus and Crescentia fled to Italy. They landed safe in Naples, and there proclaimed Christ wherever they had an opportunity. Their fervor and many miracles which they wrought attracted the attention of Emperor Diocletian to them. He ordered them to be brought before his tribunal, which being done, he at first treated them kindly, employing blandishments and making promises to induce them to renounce Christ. When this had no effect, they were cruelly tormented, but with no other result than confirming them in their constancy. Enraged, the emperor condemned them to be thrown to the wild beasts. But the lions and tigers forgot their ferocity and cowered at their feet. Now Diocletian, whose fury knew no bounds, ordered them to be cast into a caldron of molten lead and boiling pitch. They prayed, "O God, deliver us through the power of Thy name!" and behold, they remained unharmed. Thén the emperor condemned them to the rack, on which they expired, in the year 303.

LESSON

 THE heroic spirit of martyrdom exhibited by St. Vitus was owing to the early impressions of piety which he received through the teaching and example of his virtuous foster-parents. The choice of teachers, nurses, and servants who have the care of children is of the greatest importance on account of the influence they exert on them. The pagan Romans were most solicitous that no slave whose speech was not perfectly elegant and graceful should have access to children. Shall a Christian be less careful as to their virtue? It is a fatal mistake to imagine that children are too young to be infected with the contagion of vice. No age is more impressionable than childhood; no one observes more closely than the young, and nothing is so easily acquired by them as a spirit of vanity, pride, revenge, obstinacy, sloth, etc., and nothing is harder to overcome. What a happiness for a child to be formed to virtue from infancy, and to be instilled from a tender age with the spirit of piety, simplicity, meekness, and mercy! Such a foundation being well laid, the soul will easily, and sometimes without experiencing severe conflicts, rise to the height of Christian perfection.

Prayer of the Church

𝖂E BESEECH Thee, O Lord, to graciously grant us through the intercession of Thy blessed martyrs Vitus, Modestus, and Crescentia, that we may not proudly exalt ourselves, but serve Thee in humility and simplicity, so as to avoid evil and to do right for Thy sake. Through Christ our Lord. Amen.

VI

St. Christophorus, Martyr

LEGEND

𝕬N ANCIENT tradition concerning St. Christophorus relates: He was born in the land of Canaan, and was named Reprobus, that is Reprobate, for he was a barbarous heathen. In stature and strength he was a giant. Thinking no one his like in bodily vigor, he resolved to go forth in search of the mightiest master and serve him. In his wanderings, he met with a king who was praised as the most valorous man on earth. To him he offered his services and was accepted. The king was proud of his giant and kept him near his person. One day a minstrel visited the king's castle, and among the ballads he sung before the court was one on the power of Satan. At the mention of this name the

---

Note: St. Christophorus is usually called St. Christopher. He is the patron of travelers, especially motorists, and is invoked in storms and tempests. Traditional feast day: July 25.

king blessed himself, making the sign of the cross. Reprobus, wondering, asked him why he did that. The king replied: "When I make this sign, Satan has no power over me." Reprobus rejoined: "So thou fearest the power of Satan? Then he is mightier than thou, and I shall seek and serve him."

Setting forth to seek Satan, he came into a wilderness. One dark night he met a band of wild fellows riding through the forest. It was Satan and his escort. Reprobus bravely accosted him, saying he wished to serve him. He was accepted. But soon he was convinced that his new master was not the mightiest on earth. For one day, whilst approaching a crucifix by the wayside, Satan quickly took to flight, and Reprobus asked him for the reason. Satan replied: "That is the image of my greatest enemy, who conquered me on the cross. From him I always flee." When Reprobus heard this, he left the devil, and went in search of Christ.

In his wanderings, he one day came to a hut hidden in the forest. At its door sat a venerable old man. Reprobus addressed him, and in the course of the conversation that ensued the old man told him that he was a hermit, and had left the world to serve Christ, the Lord of heaven and earth. "Thou art my man," cried Reprobus; "Christ is He whom I seek, for He is the strongest and the mightiest. Tell me where I can find Him."

The hermit then began instructing the giant about God and the Redeemer, and concluded by saying: "He who would serve Christ must offer himself entirely to Him, and do and suffer everything for His sake. His reward for this will be immense and will last forever." Reprobus now asked the hermit to allow him to remain, and to continue to instruct him. The hermit consented. When Reprobus was fully instructed, he baptized him. After his baptism, a great change came over the giant. No longer proud of his great size and strength, he became meek and humble, and asked the hermit to assign to him some task by which he might serve God, his master. "For," said he, "I can not pray and fast; therefore I must serve God in some other way." The hermit led him to a broad and swift river nearby, and said: "Here build thyself a hut, and when wanderers wish to cross the river, carry them over for the love of Christ." For there was no bridge across the river.

Henceforth, day and night, whenever he was called, Reprobus faithfully performed the task assigned to him. One night he heard a child calling to be carried across the river. Quickly he rose, placed the child on his stout shoulder, took his staff and walked into the mighty current.

Arrived in midstream, the water rose higher and higher, and the child became heavier and heavier. "O child," he cried, "how heavy thou art! It seems I bear the weight of the world on my shoulder." And the child replied, "Right thou art. Thou bearest not only the world, but the Creator of heaven and earth. I am Jesus Christ, thy King and Lord, and henceforth thou shalt be called Christophorus, that is, Christ-bearer. Arrived on yonder shore, plant thy staff in the ground, and in token of my power and might tomorrow it shall bear leaves and blossoms."

And the child disappeared. On reaching the other shore, Christophorus stuck his staff into the ground, and behold, it budded forth leaves and blossoms. Then, kneeling, he promised the Lord to serve Him ever faithfully. He kept his promise, and thenceforth became a zealous preacher of the Gospel, converting many to the Faith. On his missionary peregrinations he came also to Lycia, where, after his first sermon, eighteen thousand heathens requested baptism. When Emperor Decius heard of this, he sent a company of four hundred soldiers to capture Christophorus. To these he preached so convincingly, that they all asked for baptism. Decius became enraged thereat and had him cast into prison. There he first treated him with great kindness, and surrounded him with every luxury to tempt him to sin, but in vain. Then he ordered him to be tortured in the most cruel manner, until he should deny the Faith. He was scourged, placed on plates of hot iron, boiling oil was poured over and fire was lighted under him. When all these torments did not accomplish their purpose, the soldiers were ordered to shoot him with arrows. This, too, having no effect, he was beheaded, on July 25, 254.

Two great saints refer to the wonderful achievements of St. Christophorus. St. Ambrose mentions that this saint converted forty-eight thousand souls to Christ. St. Vincent Ferrer declares that when the plague devastated Valencia, its destructive course was stayed through the intercession of St. Christophorus.

LESSON

THE legend of St. Christophorus conveys a wholesome truth. We ought all to be Christ-bearers, by preserving in our hearts faith, hope, and charity, and by receiving Our Lord worthily in Holy Communion. He alone is worthy of our service. In the service that we owe to men, we ought to serve God by doing His will. We can not divide our heart, for Our Lord Himself says, "No man can serve two masters" (*Matt.* vi. 24). If you serve the world, it deceives you, for it can not give you what it promises. If you serve

sin, Satan is your master. He, too, deceives his
servants, and leads them to perdition. Christ on
the cross conquered these two tyrants, and with
His help you can also vanquish them. Therefore,
give yourself to Him with all your heart, and
you shall find peace in this world, and eternal
bliss in the next. St. Augustine learned this
truth by sad experience, and therefore exclaims:
"Thou hast created us for Thee, O Lord, and our
heart is restless till it rests in Thee."

Prayer of the Church

GRANT us, almighty God, that whilst we celebrate the memory of Thy blessed martyr
St. Christophorus, through his intercession the
love of Thy name may be increased in us.
Through Christ our Lord. Amen.

VII

St. Dionysius, Bishop and Martyr

LEGEND

WHEN St. Paul the Apostle, in the year of Our
Lord 51, came to Athens to preach the
Gospel, he was summoned to the Areopagus, the
great council which determined all religious mat-
ters. Among the members of this illustrious as-
sembly was Dionysius. His mind had already
been prepared to receive the good tidings of the
Gospel by the miraculous darkness which over-

Note: St. Dionysius is also known as St. Denis. He is often pictured carrying his head in his hands (see p. 35). St. Denis is invoked against diabolical possession. Traditional feast day: October 9.

spread the earth at the moment of Our Lord's death on the cross. He was at that time at Heliopolis, in Egypt. On beholding the sun obscured in the midst of its course, and this without apparent cause, he is said to have exclaimed: "Either the God of nature is suffering, or the world is about to be dissolved." When St. Paul preached before the Areopagus in Athens, Dionysius easily recognized the truth and readily embraced it.*

The Apostle received him among his disciples, and appointed him bishop of the infant Church of Athens. As such he devoted himself with great zeal to the propagation of the Gospel. He made a journey to Jerusalem to visit the places hallowed by the footsteps and sufferings of our Redeemer, and there met the Apostles St. Peter and St. James, the evangelist St. Luke, and other holy apostolic men. He also had the happiness to see and converse with the Blessed Virgin Mary, and was so overwhelmed by her presence that he declared, that if he knew not Jesus to be God, he would consider her divine.

The idolatrous priests of Athens were greatly alarmed at the many conversions resulting from the eloquent preaching of Dionysius, and instigated a revolt against him. The holy bishop left Athens, and, going to Rome, visited the Pope, St. Clement. He sent him with some other holy men to Gaul. Some of his companions remained to

---

Acts 17:23-24.

Note: Gaul is present-day France.

evangelize the cities in the south, while Dionysius, with the priest Rusticus and the deacon Eleutherius continued their journey northward as far as Lutetia, the modern Paris, where the Gospel had not yet been announced. Here for many years he and his companions labored with signal success, and finally obtained the crown of martyrdom on Oct. 9, 119. Dionysius was beheaded at the advanced age of 110 years.

The spot where the three martyrs Dionysius, Rusticus, and Eleutherius suffered martyrdom is the well-known hill of Montmartre. An ancient tradition relates that St. Dionysius, after his head was severed from his body, took it up with his own hands and carried it two thousand paces to the place where, later, a church was built in his honor. The bodies of the martyrs were thrown into the river Seine, but taken up and honorably interred by a Christian lady named Catulla not far from the place where they had been beheaded. The Christians soon built a chapel on their tomb.

St. Dionysius was not only a great missionary and bishop, but also one of the most illustrious writers of the early Church. Some of his works, which are full of Catholic doctrine and Christian wisdom, are still extant, and well worthy of a convert and disciple of St. Paul, whose spirit they breathe.

Note: Many kings of France have been buried in the famous church of St. Denis (just north of Paris). St. Denis is the Apostle of France and one of the patron saints of France.

THE apostolic men like St. Dionysius, who converted so many to Christ, were filled with His spirit, and acted and lived for Him alone. They gave their lives to spread His religion, convinced that the welfare of individuals and nations depends upon it.

On religion depends the security and stability of all government and of society. Human laws are too weak to restrain those who disregard and despise the law of God. Unless a man's conscience is enlightened by religion and bound by its precepts, his passions will so far enslave him, that the impulse of evil inclinations will prompt him to every villainy of which he hopes to derive an advantage, if he can but accomplish his purpose secretly and with impunity.

True religion, on the contrary, insures comfort, peace, and happiness amid the sharpest trials, safety in death itself, and after death the most glorious and eternal reward in God. How grateful, therefore, must we be to the men who preached the true religion amid so many difficulties, trials, and persecutions; and also to those who preach it now, animated by the same spirit. And how carefully should we avoid all persons, books, and periodicals that revile and calumniate our holy Faith, and attempt its subversion!

Prayer of the Church

O GOD, who didst confer on Thy blessed servant Dionysius the virtue of fortitude in suffering, and didst join with him Rusticus and Eleutherius, to announce Thy glory to the heathens, grant, we beseech Thee, that following them, we may despise, for the love of Thee, the pleasures of this world, and that we do not recoil from its adversities. Through Christ our Lord. Amen.

VIII

St. Cyriacus, Deacon and Martyr

LEGEND

EMPEROR MAXIMIN in token of his gratitude to Diocletian, who had ceded the western half of his empire to him, ordered the building of that magnificent structure in Rome, whose ruins are still known as the "Baths of Diocletian." The Christians imprisoned for the Faith were compelled to labor under cruel overseers at this building. A zealous Christian Roman, touched with pity at this moving spectacle, resolved to employ his means in improving the condition of these poor victims of persecution.

Among the deacons of the Roman Church at that time was one by the name of Cyriacus, who was distinguished by his zeal in the performance

Note: St. Cyriacus is also called simply St. Cyriac. He is invoked in eye diseases and against diabolical possession. Traditional feast day: August 8.

of all good works. Him, with two companions,
Largus and Smaragdus, the pious Roman
selected for the execution of his plan. Cyriacus
devoted himself to the work with great ardor.
One day, whilst visiting the laborers to distribute
food amongst them, he observed a decrepit old
man, who was so feeble that he was unable to perform his severe task. Filled with pity, Cyriacus
offered to take his place. The aged prisoner con-
senting, the merciful deacon thenceforth worked
hard at the building. But after some time he was
discovered, and cast into prison. There he again
found opportunity to exercise his zeal. Some
blind men who had great confidence in the power
of his prayer, came to ask him for help in their
affliction, and he restored their sight. He and his
companions spent three years in prison, and during that time he healed many sick and converted
a great number of heathens from the darkness
of paganism.

Then Emperor Diocletian's little daughter became possessed by an evil spirit, and no one was
able to deliver her from it. To the idolatrous
priests who were called, the evil spirit declared
that he would leave the girl only when commanded to do so by Cyriacus, the deacon. He was
hastily summoned, and prayed and made the sign
of the cross over the girl, and the evil spirit departed. The emperor loved his daughter, there-

fore he was grateful to the holy deacon, and presented him with a house, where he and his companions might serve their God unmolested by their enemies.

About this time the daughter of the Persian King Sapor was attacked by a similar malady, and when he heard what Cyriacus had done for Diocletian's daughter, he wrote to the emperor, asking him to send the Christian deacon. It was done, and Cyriacus, on foot, set out for Persia. Arrived at his destination, he prayed over the girl and the evil spirit left her. On hearing of this miracle, four hundred and twenty heathens were converted to the Faith. These the saint instructed and baptized, and then set out on his homeward journey.

Returned to Rome, he continued his life of prayer and good works. But when Diocletian soon afterward left for the East, his co-emperor Maximin seized the opportunity to give vent to his hatred for the Christians, and renewed their persecution. One of the first victims was Cyriacus. He was loaded with chains and brought before the judge, who first tried blandishments and promises to induce him to renounce Christ and to sacrifice to the idols, but in vain. Then the confessor of Christ was stretched on the rack, his limbs torn from their sockets, and he was beaten with clubs. His companions

shared the same tortures. Finally, when the emperor and the judge were convinced that nothing
would shake the constancy of the holy martyrs,
they were beheaded. They gained the crown of
glory on March 16, 303.

IN THE life of St. Cyriacus two virtues shine
forth in a special manner; his love of God
and his charity toward his fellow-men. His love
of God impelled him to sacrifice all, even his life,
for His sake, thereby fulfilling the commandment: "Thou shalt love the Lord thy God with
thy whole heart, and with thy whole soul, and
with thy whole mind" (*Matt*. xxii. 37). A
greater love of God no man can have than giving
his life for Him.

St. Cyriacus also fulfilled the other commandment, of which Our Lord declared, "And the
second is like to this: Thou shalt love thy neighbor as thyself" (*Matt*. xxii. 39). He helped his
fellow-Christians to bear their burdens, relieved
them in their sufferings, assisted and encouraged
them by word and deed, and edified them by his
example. His sole aim was to do good to all men,
mindful of the words of the Royal Prophet:
"Blessed is he that understandeth concerning the
needy and the poor" (*Ps*. xl. 2). He was so imbued with the virtue of charity, that he was dis-

posed even to sacrifice his life for the relief and assistance of others.

How shall we justify our unfeeling hardness of heart, by which we seek every trifling pretense to exempt us from the duty of aiding the unfortunate? Remember the threat of the apostle, "Judgment without mercy to him that hath not done mercy" (*James* ii. 13).

Prayer of the Church

O GOD, who rejoicest us by the remembrance of Thy blessed martyrs Cyriacus, Largus, and Smaragdus; grant, we beseech Thee, that we, by celebrating their memory, may imitate their fortitude in suffering. Through Christ our Lord. Amen.

IX

St. Achatius, Martyr

LEGEND

OF THE saints named Achatius, that one is reckoned among the Holy Helpers who, as a Roman soldier, died for Christ.

Achatius was a native of Cappadocia and as a youth joined the Roman army during the reign of Emperor Hadrian, attaining the rank of captain. One day, when leading his company against the enemy, he heard a voice saying to him, "Call

Note: St. Achatius' name is also spelled Acacius. He is invoked for headaches. Traditional feast day: May 8.

on the God of Christians!" He obeyed, was instructed, and received Baptism. Filled with zeal, he henceforth sought to convert also the pagan soldiers of the army. When the emperor heard of this, Achatius was thrown into prison, then placed on the rack, bound to a post and scourged, because he refused to offer sacrifice to the idols. When all these tortures availed nothing, he was brought before the tribune Bibianus.

Asked by him what was his name and country, Achatius replied, "My name is Christian, because I am a follower of Christ; men call me Achatius. My country is Cappadocia. There my parents lived; there I was converted to the Christian faith, and was so inspired by the combats and sufferings of the Christian martyrs that I am resolved to shed my blood for Christ to attain heaven." Then Bibianus ordered him to be beaten with leaden clubs, after which he was loaded with chains and returned to the prison.

After Achatius had been in prison seven days, Bibianus was called to Byzantium, and ordered all prisoners to be transported there. On the journey Achatius suffered greatly, for his entire body was covered with wounds, his chains were galling, the guards were cruel and the roads were bad. He thought himself dying. Praying to God, a voice from the clouds answered him, "Achatius, be firm!" The soldiers of the guard were terrified and asked each other, "What is this? How can the clouds have a voice?" Many prisoners were converted. Next day some of the converts saw a number of men in shining armor speaking to Achatius, washing his wounds and healing them, so that not even a scar remained.

Arrived in Byzantium the saint was again cast into prison, and after seven days dragged before the judge. When neither promises nor the most cruel torments shook the constancy of the brave confessor of the Faith, the judge sent him to Flaccius, the proconsul of Thracia, who imprisoned him for five days, and meanwhile read the records of his former trials. Then he ordered him to be beheaded. Achatius suffered death for Christ on May 8, 311.

LESSON

ACHATIUS manfully and without fear confessed the Faith amid persecutions and sufferings. We, too, are often placed in circumstances where the profession of our Faith and the practice of the virtues inculcated by it cause us trials. But so deplorable are the effects of sensuality, avarice, and ambition, and such is the laxity and spiritual callousness of many Christians, that there is real cause for every one to be filled with alarm for the safety of his soul. It is not the crowd we are to follow, but the precepts of

the Gospel. Therefore we ought to strive to give
a good example by our faithful compliance with
the demands of religion. For Our Lord Himself
exhorts us: "So let your light shine before men,
that they may see your good works, and glorify
your Father, who is in heaven" (*Matt.* v. 16).

Prayer of the Church

O GOD, who dost give us joy through the
remembrance of Thy blessed martyrs,
Achatius and his companions; grant, we beseech
Thee, that we may be inflamed by the example
of those for whose merits we rejoice. Through
Christ our Lord. Amen.

X

St. Eustachius, Martyr

LEGEND

AT THE beginning of the second century, during the reign of Emperor Trajan, there
lived in Rome a famous general by the name of
Placidus, who was distinguished among his fellow-citizens for his wealth and military prowess.
It happened one day, that while following the
chase he became separated from his companions,
and was pursuing with eagerness a stag of extraordinary size, when suddenly it turned toward
him, and he beheld raised aloft between its antlers

Note: St. Eustachius is usually called St. Eustace (he is also called
St. Eustathius). He is invoked for protection against fire, temporal
and eternal. Traditional feast day: September 20.

the image of Jesus Christ suspended on the cross. At the same time our blessed Saviour addressed him in loving words, inviting him henceforth to follow Him by embracing the Christian faith, and to make eternal life in future the object of his pursuit.

Faithful to the grace which he had received, Placidus on his return home communicated the heavenly vision to his wife Tatiana, who informed him that she too had been favored with a heavenly apparition. Together they went immediately to the Pope, related their experience, and after due instruction received Baptism.

At the sacred font Placidus received the name of Eustachius, and his wife was called Theopista, while his sons were baptized by the names of Agapitus and Theopistus.

Upon returning to the spot where he first received the call, Eustachius was favored with another communication from Our Lord, announcing to him that he was destined to endure many and great afflictions for the sake of Christ. It was not long before his faith and patience were put to a severe trial. Stripped of all his possessions and forced to flee from the fury of the persecution, he was reduced to extreme distress, and in the course of his wanderings was by a series of calamitous events separated from his wife and children, of whom he lost all trace. For many years he dwelt in a remote spot, following the occupation of a farm laborer, until he was found by the messengers of the emperor, who was sadly in need of the skill of his former general, because a fierce war had broken out, in which the Romans sustained severe losses.

Being again invested with the command of the imperial troops, Eustachius set out for the seat of war, and achieved a decisive victory. In the course of his march he had the happiness, by a singular providence of God, to recover his wife and children, with whom he returned to Rome. His entrance into the city was attended with great rejoicings, and many were the congratulations which he received on his extraordinary good fortune. But soon afterward a solemn sacrifice of thanksgiving to the pagan deities was proclaimed, in which he was ordered by the emperor to take a part. Upon his refusal, after every effort had been made to shake his constancy, he was condemned to be exposed to the lions in the public amphitheater along with his wife and children. Finally, as the savage animals, laying aside their natural ferocity, refused to injure the confessors of Christ, Eustachius and his family were by order of the emperor enclosed in the body of an immense brazen bull, which was heated by means of a great fire enkindled beneath. The last moments of these heroic martyrs was spent in chanting the divine praises, in the midst of which their happy souls passed to the enjoyment of everlasting bliss. Their bodies, miraculously preserved uninjured, were buried with great devotion by the faithful Christians, and were afterward transferred to a magnificent church erected in their honor.

LESSON

How inspiring, to see a great man preferring justice, truth, and religion to the favor of the mighty, readily quitting estate, friends, country, and even sacrificing life, rather than consent to do violence to his conscience; and to see him, at the same time, meek, humble, patient in suffering, forgiving sincerely and loving his unjust and treacherous persecutors! Passion and revenge often beget anger and triumph over virtue and integrity. Ambition and the desire of wealth may, for a time, urge men on to brave danger, but finally they reduce them to the most abject slavery, and result in grievous crimes and misery. Religion alone is the source of charity, magnanimity, and true courage. It so enlightens the mind, as to place a man above the vicissitudes of the world; it renders him steadfast and calm in adversity, preserves him from error, teaches him to bear injustice and calumny in a tranquil spirit, and gives him that ineffable peace and joy which springs from the conviction that God's will is always most just and holy and that He protects, aids, and rewards His servants.

Does religion exert this powerful influence on us? Do we show it in our actions and conduct? Our courage and constancy must be apparent not only when we encounter danger and opposition, but also when our evil propensity urges us to yield to temptations that present sin to us in the guise of pleasure.

Prayer of the Church

O GOD, who dost permit us to celebrate the remembrance of Thy blessed martyrs, Eustachius and companions, grant us, that we may enjoy their company in eternal bliss. Through Christ our Lord. Amen.

XI

St. Giles, hermit and Abbot

LEGEND

ATHENS, in Greece, was the native city of St. Giles. He was of noble parentage, and devoted himself from early youth to piety and learning. After the death of his parents he distributed his rich inheritance to the poor, and to escape the applause of men for his charity left his country to bury himself in obscurity.

Note: St. Giles is also known as St. Aegidius. He is the patron of cripples and beggars, and is invoked against panic, epilepsy, madness and nocturnal terrors. Traditional feast day: September 1.

He sailed for France, and on his arrival there retired to a deserted country near the mouth of the river Rhone. Later he made his abode near the river Gard, and finally buried himself in a forest in the diocese of Nimes. In this solitude he passed many years, living on wild herbs and roots, with water for his drink. It is related that for some time a hind came daily to be milked by him, thus furnishing him additional sustenance. Here he lived, disengaged from earthly cares, conversing only with God, and engaged in the contemplation of heavenly things.

One day the king instituted a great hunt in the forest where Giles lived, and encountered the hind. Giving chase, the royal hunter was led to the saint's hut, where the panting animal had sought refuge. The king inquired who he was, and was greatly edified at the holiness of his life. The fame of the saintly hermit now spread far and wide, and was much increased by the many miracles wrought through his intercession. The king tried to persuade him to leave his solitude, but prevailed upon him only in so far, that Giles accepted several disciples and founded a monastery in which the rule of St. Benedict was observed, and of which he was chosen the abbot. He governed his community wisely and well, and at the earnest solicitation of his monks was ordained priest.

The fame of St. Giles' sanctity induced the Frankish King, Charles Martel to call him to his court to relieve him of a great trouble of conscience. The saint made the journey, and told the king that he would find relief and comfort only by the sincere confession of a sin which he had hitherto concealed. The king followed his advice, found interior peace and dismissed Giles with many tokens of gratitude. On his homeward journey the saint raised the recently deceased son of a nobleman to life.

After a short stay in his monastery St. Giles went to Rome, to obtain from the Pope the confirmation of some privileges and the apostolic blessing for his community. The Pope granted his wishes, and presented him, besides, with two grand and beautifully carved doors of cedar wood for his church.

St. Giles died at a ripe old age on September 1, 725. Many miracles were wrought at his tomb.

LESSON

ST. GILES left his native country and retired into solitude to escape the notice and applause of the world, and served God as a recluse. To lead such a life, there must be a special call from God. It is not suited to all, and even inconsistent with the duties of most men. But all are capable of disengaging their affections from the inordinate attachment to creatures, and of attaining to a pure and holy love of God. By making the service of God the motive of their thoughts and actions, they will sanctify their whole life.

In whatever conditions of life we may be placed, we have opportunities of subduing our evil inclinations and mortifying ourselves by frequent self-denials, of watching over our hearts and purifying our senses by recollection and prayer. Thus each one, in his station of life, may become a saint, by making his calling an exercise of virtue and his every act a step higher to perfection and eternal glory.

Prayer of the Church

O LORD, we beseech Thee to let us find grace through the intercession of Thy blessed confessor Giles; that what we can not obtain through our merits be given us through his intercession. Through Christ our Lord. Amen.

XII

St. Margaret, Virgin and Martyr

LEGEND

ST. MARGARET was the daughter of a pagan priest at Antioch. She lost her mother in infancy and was placed in the care of a nurse in the country, who was a Christian, and whose first

---

Note: St. Margaret's voice was one of the Voices heard by St. Joan of Arc. St. Margaret is invoked against backache; she is a patroness of women in childbirth. Traditional feast day: July 20.

care was to have her little charge baptized and to give the child a Christian education. Margaret grew up a modest, pious virgin, and when she returned to her father he was charmed with the grace and virtue of his daughter. He regretted only one thing; she took no part in the worship of the idols. When she told him the reason he was greatly displeased, for she stated that she was a Christian, and that nothing should separate her from the love of Christ.

Her father tried every means to change her mind, and when all his endeavors failed became enraged and drove her forth from his house. Margaret returned to her nurse and became her servant, doing all kinds of menial work, and at the same time perfecting herself in virtue.

About this time Emperor Diocletian began to persecute the Christians. One day Alybrius, the prefect of the city, saw Margaret, and fell in love with her. He sent a messenger to ask her in marriage. The pious virgin was filled with consternation at the proposal and replied to the messenger: "I can not be espoused to your master, because I am the spouse of Our Lord Jesus Christ. I am promised to Him, and to Him I wish to belong." When the prefect heard this, he became furious with rage, and gave orders to have the virgin brought to him by force. When she appeared before him he thus addressed her:

"What is your name and condition?" She replied: "I am called Margaret, and belong to a noble family. I adore Christ and serve Him." The prefect now advised her to abandon the worship of a crucified God. Margaret asked him, "How do you know that we worship a crucified God?" The prefect replied: "From the books of the Christians." Margaret continued: "Why did you not read further on? The books of the Christians would have told you that the Crucified rose on the third day, and that He ascended into heaven. Is it love of truth to believe in the abasement of Christ and to reject His glorification, when both are related in the selfsame book?"

At this reproof the prefect became angry and ordered the tender virgin to be cruelly scourged, placed on the rack, and torn with iron combs. Then she was cast into prison. There Margaret fervently thanked God for the victory she had achieved and implored His help for the combat yet in store for her. Suddenly there appeared to her the arch-enemy of mankind in the shape of a furious dragon, threatening to swallow her. The brave virgin feared him not, but made the sign of the cross, and the monster vanished. Then her desolate prison cell became suffused with heavenly light, and her heart was filled with divine consolation. At the same time her terrible wounds were suddenly healed, and not the least scar was left.

Next day Margaret was again brought before the prefect. Surprised at her complete recovery from the effects of his cruelty, he remarked that no doubt it was due to the power of the pagan gods, and exhorted her to show her gratitude to them by sacrificing to the idols. Margaret maintained that she had been healed by the power of Christ alone and declared that she despised the heathen gods. At this, the rage of Alybrius knew no bounds. He ordered lighted torches to be applied to Margaret's body, and then had her cast into icy water to intensify her torture. But scarcely had this been done when a violent earthquake occurred. Her bonds were severed and she rose unscathed from the water, without a mark of the burns caused by the flaming torches. On witnessing this miracle, a great number of spectators were converted to the Faith.

Finally the prefect ordered Margaret to be beheaded. Her glorious martyrdom and death occurred about the year 275.

LESSON

T HE history of the virgin martyr St. Margaret teaches us that we can and ought to serve God even in youth. In the Old Law God commanded all the first-born and the first-fruits to be offered to Him. "Thou shalt not delay to pay thy tithes and first-fruits. Thou shalt give the first-born of thy sons to Me" (*Ex.* xxii. 29).

Certainly our whole life ought to be dedicated to the service of God; but from the above command we are to understand that God especially desires our service during the early years of our life. They are our first-fruits. St. Augustine calls the years of youth the blossoms, the most beautiful flowers of life, and St. Thomas Aquinas writes: "What the young give to God in their early years, they give of the bloom, of the full vigor and beauty of life."

Youth is the age beset with countless temptations. Safety is found only in the service of God, by obedience, humility, and docility. This is not so difficult as it appears, and Our Lord Himself invites you to His service, saying: "My son, give Me thy heart" (*Prov.* xxiii. 26), and, "Taste and see that the Lord is sweet" (*Ps.* xxxiii. 9).

Prayer of the Church

WE BESEECH Thee, O Lord, grant us Thy favor through the intercession of Thy blessed virgin and martyr Margaret, who pleased Thee by the merit of her purity and by the confession of Thy might. Through Christ our Lord. Amen.

XIII

St. Catherine, Virgin and Martyr

LEGEND

St. Catherine was a native of Alexandria, Egypt, a city then famous for its schools of philosophy. She was a daughter of Costis, half-brother of Constantine, and of Sabinella, queen of Egypt. Her wisdom and acquirements were remarkable, the philosophy of Plato being her favorite study. While Catherine was yet young her father died, leaving her heiress to the kingdom. Her love of study and retirement displeased her subjects, who desired her to marry, asserting that her gifts of noble birth, wealth, beauty, and knowledge should be transmitted to her children.

The princess replied that the husband whom she would wed must be even more richly endowed than herself. His blood must be the noblest, his rank must surpass her own, his beauty without comparison, his benignity great enough to forgive all offences. The people of Alexandria were disheartened, for they knew of no such prince; but Catherine remained persistent in her determination to wed none other.

Now, it happened that a certain hermit who lived near Alexandria had a vision in which he saw the Blessed Virgin, who sent him to tell

Note: The voice of St. Catherine was one of the voices heard by St. Joan of Arc. St. Catherine is patroness of Christian philosophers, of maidens, preachers, wheelwrights and mechanics; she is also invoked by students, orators, barristers, etc. Traditional feast: Nov. 25.

Catherine that her divine Son was the Spouse whom she desired. He alone possessed all, and more, than the requirements she demanded. The holy man gave Catherine a picture of Jesus and Mary; and when the princess had gazed upon the face of Christ she loved Him so that she could think of naught else, and the studies in which she had been wont to take delight became distasteful to her.

One night Catherine dreamed that she accompanied the hermit to a sanctuary, whence angels came to meet her. She fell on her face before them, but one of the angelic band bade her, "Rise dear sister Catherine, for the King of glory delighteth to honor thee." She rose and followed the angels to the presence of the queen of heaven, who was surrounded by angels and saints and was beautiful beyond description. The queen welcomed her and led her to her divine Son, Our Lord. But He turned from her, saying: "She is not fair and beautiful enough for Me."

Catherine awoke at these words and wept bitterly until morning. She then sent for the hermit and inquired what would make her worthy of the heavenly Bridegroom. The saintly recluse instructed her in the true Faith and, with her mother, she was baptized. That night, in a dream, the Blessed Virgin and her divine Son again appeared to her. Mary presented her to

Jesus, saying: "Behold, she has been regenerated in the water of Baptism." Then Christ smiled on her and plighted His troth to her by putting a ring on her finger. When she awoke the ring was still there, and thenceforth Catherine despised all earthly things and longed only for the hour when she should go to her heavenly Bridegroom.

After the death of Sabinella, Emperor Maximin came to Alexandria and declared a persecution against the Christians. Catherine appeared in the temple and held an argument with the tyrant, utterly confounding him. The emperor ordained that fifty of the most learned men of the empire be brought to dispute with her; but, sustained by the power of God, Catherine not only vanquished them in argument, but converted them to the true Faith. In his fury Maximin commanded that the new Christians be burned; and Catherine comforted them, since they could not be baptized, by telling them that their blood should be their baptism and the flames their crown of glory.

The emperor then tried other means to overcome the virtue of the noble princess; but, failing to do this, he ordered her to be cast into a dungeon and starved to death. Twelve days later, when the dungeon was opened, a bright light and fragrant perfume filled it, and Catherine, who had been nourished by angels, came forth radiant and beautiful. On seeing this miracle, the empress and many noble Alexandrians declared themselves Christians, and suffered death at the command of the emperor.

Catherine was not spared, for Maximin made a further attempt to win her. He offered to make her mistress of the world if she would but listen to him, and when she still spurned his proposals, he ordered her to the torture. She was bound to four spiked wheels which revolved in different directions, that she might be torn into many pieces. But an angel consumed the wheels by fire, and the fragments flying around killed the executioners and many of the spectators. The tyrant then ordered her to be scourged and beheaded. The sentence was carried into effect on November 25, 307.

A pious legend, recognized by the Church, says that angels bore Catherine's body to Mount Sinai, and buried it there.

LESSON

St. Catherine, for her erudition and the spirit of piety by which she sanctified it, was chosen the model and patroness of Christian philosophers.

Learning, next to virtue, is the noblest quality and ornament of the human mind. Profane science teaches many useful truths, but when compared with the importance of the study of the science of the saints, they are of value only inasmuch as when made subservient to the latter. The study of the saints was to live in the spirit of Christ. This science is taught by the Church, and acquired by listening to her instructions, by pious reading and meditation.

Be intent on learning this science, and order your life according to its rules. It is the "one thing necessary," for it is the foundation of all wisdom and true happiness. "The fear of the Lord is the beginning of wisdom"(*Ps.* cx. 10).

Prayer of the Church

O GOD, who didst give the law to Moses on the summit of Mount Sinai, and by the holy angels didst miraculously transfer there the body of blessed Catherine, virgin and martyr; grant us, we beseech Thee, to come, through her intercession, to the mountain which is Christ. Through the same Christ our Lord. Amen.

XIV

St. Barbara, Virgin and Martyr

LEGEND

NICOMEDIA, a city in Asia Minor, was St. Barbara's birthplace. Her father Dioscurus was a pagan. Fearing that his only child might

---

Note: St. Barbara is the patroness of architects, builders, miners and artillerymen, and she is invoked against lightning, fire and sudden death. Traditional feast day: December 4.

learn to know and love the doctrines of Christianity, he shut her up in a tower, apart from all intercourse with others. Nevertheless Barbara became a Christian. She passed her time in study, and from her lonely tower she used to watch the heavens in their wondrous beauty. She soon became convinced that the "heavens were telling the glory of God," a God greater than the idols she had been taught to worship. Her desire to know that God was in itself a prayer which He answered in His own wise way.

The fame of Origen, that famous Christian teacher in Alexandria, reached even the remote tower, and Barbara sent a trusty servant with the request that he would make known to her the truth. Origen sent her one of his disciples, disguised as a physician, who instructed and baptized her. She practised her new religion discreetly while waiting for a favorable opportunity of acquainting her father with her conversion.

This opportunity came in a short time. Some workmen were sent by Dioscurus to make another room in the tower, and when they had made two windows she directed them to make a third. When her father saw this additional window, he asked the reason for it. She replied, "Know, my father, that the soul receives light through three windows, the Father, the Son, and the Holy

Ghost, and the three are one." The father became so angry at this discovery of her having become a Christian, that he would have killed his daughter with his sword, had she not fled to the top of the tower. He followed her, and finally had her in his power. First he wreaked his vengeance on her in blows, then clutching her by the hair he dragged her away and thrust her into a hut to prevent her escape. Next he tried every means to induce her to renounce her faith; threats, severe punishments, and starvation had no effect on the constancy of the Christian maiden.

Finding himself powerless to shake his daughter's constancy, Dioscurus delivered her to the proconsul Marcian, who had her scourged and tortured, but without causing her to deny the Faith. During her sufferings, her father stood by, exulting in the torments of his child. Next night, after she had been taken back to prison, Our Lord appeared to her and healed her wounds. When Barbara appeared again before him, Marcian was greatly astonished to find no trace of the cruelties that had been perpetrated on her body. Again she resisted his importunities to deny the Faith, and when he saw that all his efforts were in vain, he pronounced the sentence of death. Barbara was to be beheaded. Her unnatural father claimed the privilege to execute it with his own hands, and with one blow severed his daughter's head from her body, on December 4, 237.

At the moment of the saint's death a great tempest arose and Dioscurus was killed by lightning. Marcian, too, was overtaken by the same fate.

LESSON

SINCE early times St. Barbara is invoked as the patroness against lightning and explosions, and is called upon by those who desire the sacraments of the dying in their last illness, and many are the instances of the efficacy of her intercession.

We all wish for a happy and blessed death. To attain it, we must make the preparation for it the great object of our life; we must learn to die to the world and to ourselves, and strive after perfection in virtue. There is no greater comfort in adversity, no more powerful incentive to withdrawing our affections from this world, than to remember the blessing of a happy death. Well prepared, death may strike us in any form whatsoever, and however suddenly, it will find us ready.

We can be guilty of no greater folly than to delay our preparation for death, repentance, the reception of the sacraments, and the amendment of our life, from day to day, from the time of health to the time of illness, and in illness to the very last moments, thinking that even then we can obtain pardon. St. Augustine observes: "It is very dangerous to postpone the performance of a duty on which our whole eternity depends to the most inconvenient time, the last hour." And St. Bernard remarks: "In Holy Scripture we find one single instance of one who received pardon at the last moment. He was the thief crucified with Jesus. He is alone, that you despair not; he is alone, also, that you sin not by presumption on God's mercy." If you, therefore, wish for a happy death, prepare for it in time.

Prayer of the Church

O GOD, who among the wonders of Thy might didst grant the victory of martyrdom also to the weaker sex, graciously grant us that we, by recalling the memory of Thy blessed virgin and martyr Barbara, through her example may be led to Thee. Through Christ our Lord. Amen.

PART II

Novenas to the Holy Helpers

Prayers and Petitions

"In every thing by prayer and supplication with thanksgiving let your petitions be made known to God" (*Philipp.* iv. 6).

Rules for the Proper Observance of Novenas

By St. Alphonsus Liguori

1. THE soul must be in the state of grace; for the devotion of a sinful heart pleases neither God nor the saints.

2. We must persevere, that is, the prayers for each day of the novena must never be omitted.

3. If possible, we should visit a church every day, and there implore the favor we desire.

4. Every day we ought to perform certain specified acts of exterior self-denial and interior mortification, in order to prepare us thereby for the reception of grace.

5. It is most important that we receive holy communion when making a novena. Therefore prepare yourself well for it.

6. After obtaining the desired grace for which the novena was made, do not omit to return thanks to God and to the saint through whose intercession your prayers were heard.

Note: A novena is made by praying some prayer or prayers for nine days in succession.

Novena to Each of the Holy Helpers

For Each of the Following Novenas

ALMIGHTY and eternal God! With lively faith and reverently worshiping Thy divine Majesty, I prostrate myself before Thee and invoke with filial trust Thy supreme bounty and mercy. Illumine the darkness of my intellect with a ray of Thy heavenly light and inflame my heart with the fire of Thy divine love, that I may contemplate the great virtues and merits of the saint in whose honor I make this novena, and following his example imitate, like him, the life of Thy divine Son.

Moreover, I beseech Thee to grant graciously, through the merits and intercession of this powerful Helper, the petition which through him I humbly place before Thee, devoutly saying, "Thy will be done on earth as it is in heaven." Vouchsafe graciously to hear it, if it redounds to Thy greater glory and to the salvation of my soul. Amen.

I

Novena in honor of St. George

Preparatory Prayer (p. 67).

PRAYER IN HONOR OF ST. GEORGE

O GOD, who didst grant to St. George strength
and constancy in the various torments
which he sustained for our holy faith; we beseech Thee to preserve, through his intercession,
our faith from wavering and doubt, so that we
may serve Thee with a sincere heart faithfully
unto death. Through Christ our Lord. Amen.

INVOCATION OF ST. GEORGE

FAITHFUL servant of God and invincible martyr, St. George; favored by God with the gift
of faith, and inflamed with an ardent love of
Christ, thou didst fight valiantly against the dragon
of pride, falsehood, and deceit. Neither pain nor
torture, sword nor death could part thee from the
love of Christ. I fervently implore thee for the
sake of this love to help me by thy intercession to
overcome the temptations that surround me, and
to bear bravely the trials that oppress me, so that
I may patiently carry the cross which is placed
upon me; and let neither distress nor difficulties
separate me from the love of Our Lord Jesus
Christ. Valiant champion of the Faith, assist me

in the combat against evil, that I may win the crown promised to them that persevere unto the end.

Prayer

MY LORD and my God! I offer up to Thee my petition in union with the bitter passion and death of Jesus Christ, Thy Son, together with the merits of His immaculate and blessed Mother, Mary ever virgin, and of all the saints, particularly with those of the holy Helper in whose honor I make this novena.

Look down upon me, merciful Lord! Grant me Thy grace and Thy love, and graciously hear my prayer. Amen.

II

Novena in Honor of St. Blase

Preparatory Prayer (p. 67).

PRAYER IN HONOR OF ST. BLASE

O GOD, deliver us through the intercession of Thy holy bishop and martyr Blase, from all evil of soul and body, especially from all ills of the throat; and grant us the grace to make a good confession in the confident hope of obtaining Thy pardon, and ever to praise with worthy lips Thy most holy name. Through Christ our Lord. Amen.

INVOCATION OF ST. BLASE

ST. BLASE, gracious benefactor of mankind and faithful servant of God, who for the love of our Saviour didst suffer so many tortures with patience and resignation; I invoke thy powerful intercession. Preserve me from all evils of soul and body. Because of thy great merits God endowed thee with the special grace to help those that suffer from ills of the throat; relieve and preserve me from them, so that I may always be able to fulfil my duties, and with the aid of God's grace perform good works. I invoke thy help as special physician of souls, that I may confess my sins sincerely in the holy sacrament of Penance and obtain their forgiveness. I recommend to thy merciful intercession also those who unfortunately concealed a sin in confession. Obtain for them the grace to accuse themselves sincerely and contritely of the sin they concealed, of the sacrilegious confessions and communions they made, and of all the sins they committed since then, so that they may receive pardon, the grace of God, and the remission of the eternal punishment. Amen.

Prayer (p. 69).

III

Preparatory Prayer (p. 67).

PRAYER IN HONOR OF ST. ERASMUS

O GOD, grant us through the intercession of Thy dauntless bishop and martyr Erasmus, who so valiantly confessed the Faith, that we may learn the doctrine of this faith, practise its precepts, and thereby be made worthy to attain its promises. Through Christ our Lord. Amen.

INVOCATION OF ST. ERASMUS

HOLY martyr Erasmus, who didst willingly and bravely bear the trials and sufferings of life, and by thy charity didst console many fellow-sufferers; I implore thee to remember me in my needs and to intercede for me with God. Staunch confessor of the Faith, victorious vanquisher of all tortures, pray Jesus for me and ask Him to grant me the grace to live and die in the Faith through which thou didst obtain the crown of glory. Amen.

Prayer (p. 69).

IV

Preparatory Prayer (p. 67).

PRAYER IN HONOR OF ST. PANTALEON

O GOD, who didst give to St. Pantaleon the grace of exercising charity toward his fellow-men by distributing his goods to the poor, and hast made him a special patron of the sick, grant that we, too, show our charity by works of mercy; and through the intercession of this Thy servant preserve us from sickness. But if it be Thy will that illness should afflict us, give us the grace to bear it patiently, and let it promote our soul's salvation. Amen.

INVOCATION OF ST. PANTALEON

ST. PANTALEON, who during life didst have great pity for the sick and with the help of God didst often relieve and cure them; I invoke thy intercession with God, that I may obtain the grace to serve Him in good health by cheerfully fulfilling the duties of my state of life. But if it be His holy will to visit me with illness, pain, and suffering, do thou aid me with thy powerful prayer to submit humbly to His chastisements, to accept sickness in the spirit of penance and to bear it patiently according to His holy will. Amen.

Prayer (p. 69).

V

Preparatory Prayer (p. 67).

Novena in honor of St. Vitus

PRAYER IN HONOR OF ST. VITUS

GRANT us, O God, through the intercession of St. Vitus, a due estimation of the value of our soul and of its redemption by the precious blood of Thy Son Jesus Christ; so that, for its salvation, we bear all trials with fortitude. Give this Thy youthful servant and heroic martyr as a guide and protector to Christian youths, that following his example they may after a victorious combat receive the crown of justice in heaven. Through Christ our Lord. Amen.

INVOCATION OF ST. VITUS

ST. VITUS, glorious martyr of Christ; in thy youth thou wast exposed to violent and dangerous temptations, but in the fear of God and for the love of Jesus thou didst victoriously overcome them. O amiable, holy youth, I implore thee by the love of Jesus, assist me with thy powerful intercession to overcome the temptations to evil, to avoid every occasion of sin, and thus to preserve spotless the robe of innocence and sanctifying grace, and to bring it unstained to the judgment-seat of Jesus Christ, that I may forever enjoy the beatific vision of God which is promised to the pure of heart. Amen.

Prayer (p. 69).

VI

Novena in honor of St. Christophorus

Preparatory Prayer (p. 67).

PRAYER IN HONOR OF ST. CHRISTOPHORUS

O GOD, who didst make St. Christophorus a true Christ-bearer who converted multitudes to the Christian faith, and who didst give him the grace to suffer for Thy sake the most cruel torments; through the intercession of this saint we implore Thee to protect us from sin, the only real evil. Preserve us, also, against harmful elementary forces, such as earthquake, lightning, fire, and flood. Amen.

INVOCATION OF ST. CHRISTOPHORUS

GREAT St. Christophorus, seeking the strongest and mightiest master thou didst find him in Jesus Christ, the almighty God of heaven and earth, and didst faithfully serve Him with all thy power to the end of thy life, gaining for Him countless souls and finally shedding thy blood for Him; obtain for me the grace to bear Christ always in my heart, as thou didst once bear Him on thy shoulder, so that I thereby may be strength-

Note: St. Christophorus is usually called St. Christopher.

ened to overcome victoriously all temptations and
resist all enticements of the world, the flesh, and
the devil, and that the powers of darkness may
not prevail against me.   Amen.

Prayer (p. 69).

VII

Novena in honor of St. Dionysius

Preparatory Prayer (p. 67).

PRAYER IN HONOR OF ST. DIONYSIUS

O GOD, who didst confer Thy saving faith on
the people of France through Thy holy bishop
and martyr Dionysius, and didst glorify him before and after his martyrdom by many miracles;
grant us through his intercession that the Faith
practised and preached by him be our light on
the way of life, so that we may be preserved from
all anxieties of conscience, and if by human
frailty we have sinned, we may return to Thee
speedily by true penance.   Through Christ our
Lord.   Amen.

INVOCATION OF ST. DIONYSIUS

GLORIOUS servant of God, St. Dionysius, with
intense love thou didst devote thyself to
Christ after learning to know Him through the
apostle St. Paul, and didst preach His saving

Note: St. Dionysius is also called St. Denis.

name to the nations, to bring whom to His knowledge and love thou didst not shrink from martyrdom; implore for me a continual growth in the knowledge and love of Jesus, so that my restless heart may experience that peace which He alone can give. Help me by thy powerful intercession with God to serve Him with a willing heart, to devote myself with abiding love to His service, and thereby to attain the eternal bliss of heaven. Amen.

Prayer (p. 69).

VIII

Novena in honor of St. Cyriacus

Preparatory Prayer (p. 67).

PRAYER IN HONOR OF ST. CYRIACUS

O God, who didst grant to St. Cyriacus the grace of heroic charity and trustful resignation to Thy holy will; bestow upon us, through his intercession, the grace to walk before Thee in self-denying charity and to know and fulfil Thy will in all things. Through Christ our Lord. Amen.

INVOCATION OF ST. CYRIACUS

St. Cyriacus, great servant of God, loving Christ with all thy heart, thou didst for His sake also love thy fellow-men, and didst serve them even at the peril of thy life, for which charity God rewarded thee with the power to overcome Satan, the arch-enemy, and to deliver the poor obsessed from his dreadful tyranny; implore for me of God an effective, real, and true charity. Show thy power over Satan also in me; deliver me from his influence when he tries to tempt me. Help me to repel his assaults and to gain the victory over him in life and in death. Amen.

Prayer (p. 69).

IX

Novena in honor of St. Achatius

Preparatory Prayer (p. 67).

PRAYER IN HONOR OF ST. ACHATIUS

O GOD, who didst fortify Thy holy martyr Achatius with constancy and trustful reliance on Thee in death; grant us through his intercession at the hour of our death to be free from all anxiety and victorious in our last combat with the enemy. Through Christ our Lord. Amen.

INVOCATION OF ST. ACHATIUS

VALIANT martyr of Christ, St. Achatius, who preached Christ faithfully before kings and judges, and didst gain the victory over the ene-

mies of God; help me through thy powerful intercession to resist and gain the victory over all the
enemies of my salvation, over the world and its
allurements, over the concupiscence of the flesh,
and over the temptations of Satan. I implore thee
particularly to assist me in my agony, when the
powers of hell rise against me to rob my soul.
Then do thou come to my aid and repel the assaults of the enemy, so that I surrender my soul
into the hands of my Redeemer in faith, hope, and
charity, and confiding in His infinite merits.
Through the same Christ our Lord.   Amen.

Prayer (p. 69).

X

Novena in Honor of St. Eustachius

Preparatory Prayer (p. 67).

PRAYER IN HONOR OF ST. EUSTACHIUS

O GOD, who didst lead Thy holy martyr Eustachius safely through many trials and dangers to the glorious crown of martyrdom; en-
lighten and strengthen us through his intercession, that we persevere in Thy love amid the
trials of this life, and by resignation to Thy
holy will come forth from the darkness of
this earth into the light of Thy eternal glory.
Amen.

Note: St. Eustachius is usually called St. Eustace.

INVOCATION OF ST. EUSTACHIUS

ᕼEROIC servant of God, St. Eustachius, cast from the height of earthly glory and power into the deepest misery, thou wast engaged for a long time in the labor of a menial servant, eating the bitter bread of destitution; but never didst thou murmur against the severe probation to which God subjected thee. I implore thee to aid me with thy powerful intercession, that in all conditions I may resign myself to the holy will of God, and particularly that I may bear poverty and its consequences with patience, trusting in God's providence, completely resigned to the decrees of Him who humbles and exalts, chastises and heals, sends trials and consolations, and who has promised to those who follow Him in the spirit of poverty His beatific vision throughout all eternity. Amen.

Prayer (p. 69).

XI

Novena in honor of St. Giles

Preparatory Prayer (p. 67).

PRAYER IN HONOR OF ST. GILES

O GOD, we beseech Thee to grant us, through the merits and intercession of St. Giles, to flee from the vanity and praise of this world, to avoid carefully all occasions of sin, to cleanse our hearts from all wickedness by a sincere confession, to leave this world in Thy love and rich in good works, and to find Thee gracious on the day of judgment. Through Christ our Lord. Amen.

INVOCATION OF ST. GILES

ZEALOUS follower of Christ, St. Giles; from early youth thou didst take to heart the words of our Saviour: "Learn of Me, because I am meek and humble of heart." Therefore thou didst flee from the praise and honors of the world, and wast rewarded with the grace to preserve thy heart from all sin and to persevere in a holy life to a ripe old age. I, on my part, through pride, self-confidence, and negligence, yielded to my evil inclinations, and thereby sinned grievously and often, offending my God and Lord, my Creator and Redeemer, my most loving Father. Therefore I implore thee to help me through thy mighty intercession to be enlightened by the Holy Ghost, that I may know the malice, grievousness, and multitude of my sins, confess them humbly, fully, and contritely, and receive pardon, tranquillity of heart, and peace of conscience from God. Amen.

Prayer (p. 69).

XII

Preparatory Prayer (p. 67).

PRAYER IN HONOR OF ST. MARGARET

O God, grant us through the intercession of Thy holy virgin and martyr Margaret, undauntedly to confess the Faith, carefully to observe the chastity of our state of life, and to overcome the temptations of the world, the flesh, and the devil, and thereby escape the punishments of eternal damnation. Amen.

INVOCATION OF ST. MARGARET

St. Margaret, holy virgin and martyr, thou didst faithfully preserve the robe of holy innocence and purity, valiantly resisting all the blandishments and allurements of the world for the love of thy divine Spouse, Jesus Christ; help me to overcome all temptations against the choicest of all virtues, holy purity, and to remain steadfast in the love of Christ, in order to preserve this great gift of God. Implore for me the grace of perseverance in prayer, distrust of myself, and flight from the occasions of sin, and finally the grace of a good death, so that in heaven I may "follow the Lamb whithersoever He goeth." Amen.

Prayer (p. 69).

XIII

Preparatory Prayer (p. 67).

PRAYER IN HONOR OF ST. CATHERINE

O GOD, who didst distinguish Thy holy virgin and martyr Catherine by the gift of great wisdom and virtue, and a victorious combat with the enemies of the Faith; grant us, we beseech Thee, through her intercession, constancy in the Faith and the wisdom of the saints, that we may devote all the powers of our mind and heart to Thy service. Through Christ our Lord. Amen.

INVOCATION OF ST. CATHERINE

St. CATHERINE, glorious virgin and martyr, resplendent in the luster of wisdom and purity; thy wisdom refuted the adversaries of divine truth and covered them with confusion; thy immaculate purity made thee a spouse of Christ, so that after thy glorious martyrdom angels carried thy body to Mount Sinai. Implore for me progress in the science of the saints and the virtue of holy purity, that vanquishing the enemies of my soul, I may be victorious in my last combat and after death be conducted by the angels into the eternal beatitude of heaven. Amen.

Prayer (p. 69).

XIV

Novena in Honor of St. Barbara

Preparatory Prayer (p. 67).

PRAYER IN HONOR OF ST. BARBARA

O GOD, who didst adorn Thy holy virgin and martyr Barbara with extraordinary fortitude in the confession of the Faith, and didst console her in the most atrocious torments; grant us through her intercession perseverance in the fulfilment of Thy law and the grace of being fortified before our end with the holy sacraments, and of a happy death. Through Christ our Lord. Amen.

INVOCATION OF ST. BARBARA

INTREPID virgin and martyr, St. Barbara, through thy intercession come to my aid in all needs of my soul. Obtain for me the grace to be preserved from a sudden and unprovided death; assist me in my agony, when my senses are benumbed and I am in the throes of death. Then, O powerful patroness of the dying, come to my aid! Repel from me all the assaults and temptations of the evil one, and obtain for me the grace to receive before death the holy sacraments, that I breathe forth my soul confirmed in faith, hope, and charity, and be worthy to enter eternal glory. Amen.

St. Barbara, at my last end
  Obtain for me the Sacrament;
Assist one in that direst need
  When I my God and Judge must meet:
That robed in sanctifying grace
  My soul may stand before His face.

Prayer (p. 69).

Novena to All the Fourteen Holy Helpers

PREPARATORY PRAYER

(By St. Alphonsus Liguori.)

GREAT princes of heaven, Holy Helpers, who sacrificed to God all your earthly possessions, wealth, preferment, and even life, and who now are crowned in heaven in the secure enjoyment of eternal bliss and glory; have compassion on me, a poor sinner in this vale of tears, and obtain for me from God, for whom you gave up all things and who loves you as His servants, the strength to bear patiently all the trials of this life, to overcome all temptations, and to persevere in God's service to the end, that one day I too may be received into your company, to praise and glorify Him, the supreme Lord, whose beatific vision you enjoy, and whom you praise and glorify for ever. Amen.

FIRST DAY

The Devotion to the Fourteen Holy Helpers

Preparatory Prayer (p. 85).

MEDITATION

THE practice of honoring and invoking the saints to obtain, through their intercession, help in the various needs of body and soul, is as old as the Church. At what period, however, the custom of having recourse to the fourteen saints called Holy Helpers originated, is unknown. Nevertheless it is certain that each one of them was invoked for his intercession with God since his entrance into heaven. Prayer is the Christian's resource in every difficulty: and difficulties and trials are never wanting on earth.

Because the needs of mankind on earth are various, the faithful selected certain saints as intercessors in certain cases of distress, and obtained relief; hence these saints came to be regarded as special patrons in such trials, and were called Holy Helpers.

PRACTICE

MAKE this novena with full confidence in the power of the intercession of the Fourteen Holy Helpers. During their earthly life they devoted their whole energy to the spreading of

God's kingdom and the relief and succor of their fellow-men. Much more efficiently can they do so now when they are in the enjoyment of eternal happiness, and can supplicate for us at the very throne of God.

The saints *can* help us through their intercession. God hears their prayers and He wrought miracles to confirm us in this belief, even whilst His servants sojourned here on earth. They *desire* and are willing to help us. St. Bernard says: "In heaven hearts do not grow cold; they are rather rendered more affectionate and tender. By receiving the crown of justice the saints were not hardened against the sufferings of their brethren on earth."

Therefore, in calling on them, have full confidence in their power and ability to come to your aid.

Prayer

WE BESEECH Thee, O Lord, to hear the prayer which we send up to Thee in honor of Thy glorified servants, the Fourteen Holy Helpers: and as we can not rely upon our own justice, grant our petition through the intercession of those whose merits have made them especially dear to Thee. Through Christ our Lord. Amen.

Litany of the Fourteen Holy Helpers[1]

Lord, have mercy on us.
    Christ, have mercy on us.
Lord, have mercy on us.   Christ, hear us.
    Christ, graciously hear us.

God the Father of heaven,[2]
God the Son, Redeemer of the world,
God the Holy Ghost,
Holy Trinity, one God,

Holy Mary, queen of martyrs,[3]
St. Joseph, helper in all needs,
Fourteen Holy Helpers,
St. George, valiant martyr of Christ,
St. Blase, zealous bishop and benefactor of the
    poor,
St. Erasmus, mighty protector of the oppressed,
St. Pantaleon, miraculous exemplar of charity,
St. Vitus, special protector of chastity,
St. Christophorus, mighty intercessor in dangers,
St. Dionysius, shining mirror of faith and con-
    fidence,
St. Cyriacus, terror of hell,
St. Achatius, helpful advocate in death,
St. Eustachius, exemplar of patience in adversity,
St. Giles, despiser of the world,

[1]For private devotion.   [3]Pray for us.
[2]Have mercy on us.

St. Margaret, valiant champion of the Faith,[1]
St. Catherine, victorious defender of the Faith
   and of purity,
St. Barbara, mighty patroness of the dying,
All ye Holy Helpers,
All ye saints of God,
In temptations against faith,
In adversity and trials,
In anxiety and want,
In every combat,
In every temptation,
In sickness,
In all needs,
In fear and terror,
In dangers of salvation,
In dangers of honor,
In dangers of reputation,
In dangers of property,
In dangers by fire and water,
Be merciful, spare us, O Lord!
Be merciful, graciously hear us, O Lord!

From all sin,[2]
From Thy wrath,
From the scourge of earthquake,
From plague, famine, and war,
From lightning and storms,
From a sudden and unprovided **death,**
From eternal damnation,

[1]Pray for us.
[2]Deliver us, O Lord.

Through the mystery of Thy holy incarnation,[1]
Through Thy birth and Thy life,
Through Thy cross and passion,
Through Thy death and burial,
Through the merits of Thy blessed Mother Mary,
Through the merits of the Fourteen Holy Helpers,
On the Day of Judgment, deliver us, O Lord!

We sinners, beseech Thee hear us.
That Thou spare us,[2]
That Thou pardon us,
That Thou convert us to true penance,
That Thou give and preserve the fruits of the earth,
That Thou protect and propagate Thy holy Church,
That Thou preserve peace and concord among the nations,
That Thou give eternal rest to the souls of the departed,
That Thou come to our aid through the intercession of the Holy Helpers,
That through the intercession of St. George Thou preserve us in the Faith,
That through the intercession of St. Blase Thou confirm us in hope,
That through the intercession of St. Erasmus Thou enkindle in us Thy holy love,

[1] Deliver us, O Lord.
[2] We beseech Thee, hear us.

That through the intercession of St. Pantaleon
Thou give us charity for our neighbor,

That through the intercession of St. Vitus Thou
teach us the value of our soul,

That through the intercession of St. Christophorus Thou preserve us from sin,

That through the intercession of St. Dionysius
Thou give us tranquillity of conscience,

That through the intercession of St. Cyriacus
Thou grant us resignation to Thy holy will,

That through the intercession of St. Eustachius
Thou give us patience in adversity,

That through the intercession of St. Achatius
Thou grant us a happy death,

That through the intercession of St. Giles Thou
grant us a merciful judgment,

That through the intercession of St. Margaret
Thou preserve us from hell,

That through the intercession of St. Catherine
Thou shorten our purgatory,

That through the intercession of St. Barbara
Thou receive us in heaven,

That through the intercession of all the Holy
Helpers Thou wilt grant our prayers,

Lamb of God, who takest away the sins of the
world, spare us, O Lord.

Lamb of God, who takest away the sins of the
world, graciously hear us, O Lord.

Lamb of God, who takest away the sins of the
world, have mercy on us, O Lord.

V. Pray for us, ye Fourteen Holy Helpers.

R. That we may be made worthy of the promise of Christ.

Let us Pray

ALMIGHTY and eternal God, who hast bestowed extraordinary graces and gifts on Thy saints George, Blase, Erasmus, Pantaleon, Vitus, Christophorus, Dionysius, Cyriacus, Eustachius, Achatius, Giles, Margaret, Catherine, and Barbara, and hast illustrated them by miracles; we beseech Thee to graciously hear the petitions of all who invoke their intercession. Through Christ our Lord. Amen.

O God, who didst miraculously fortify the Fourteen Holy Helpers in the confession of the Faith; grant us, we beseech Thee, to imitate their fortitude in overcoming all temptations against it, and protect us through their intercession in all dangers of soul and body, so that we may serve Thee in purity of heart and chastity of body. Through Christ our Lord. Amen.

INVOCATION OF THE HOLY HELPERS

FOURTEEN Holy Helpers, who served God in humility and confidence on earth and are now in the enjoyment of His beatific vision in heaven; because you persevered till death you gained the crown of eternal life. Remember the dangers that surround us in this vale of tears, and intercede for us in all our needs and adversities. Amen.

Fourteen Holy Helpers, select friends of God, I honor you as mighty intercessors, and come with filial confidence to you in my needs, for the relief of which I have undertaken to make this novena. Help me by your intercession to placate God's wrath, which I have provoked by my sins, and aid me in amending my life and doing penance. Obtain for me the grace to serve God with a willing heart, to be resigned to His holy will, to be patient in adversity and to persevere unto the end, so that, having finished my earthly course, I may join you in heaven, there to praise for ever God, who is wonderful in His saints. Amen.

SECOND DAY

The Destiny of Man

Preparatory Prayer (p. 85).

MEDITATION

THE Holy Helpers faithfully co-operated with God's designs concerning their eternal destiny. No obstacle could prevail on them to stray from the path of duty. Always and everywhere they fulfilled the will of God.

You, too, have an eternal destiny. You are not your own master, but belong to God, whose servant and property you are. Therefore you must obey Him, and not your own inclinations; you must do His will, and not your own. God had the right of requiring our submission to Him without giving us a reward, because He is Our Lord; nevertheless He promised to give us Himself in reward for our faithful service. Ought this not be sufficient inducement for us to serve Him zealously and gratefully?

Remember, moreover, that you shall be unhappy both in this and in the next world if you do not give yourself entirely to God, for whom you were created. St. Augustine says: "Thou hast created us for Thee, O Lord, and our heart remains restless till it rests in Thee."

PRACTICE

THANK God for the undeserved grace of creation and redemption. Make an act of contrition for having served Him so negligently. Promise amendment, and invoke the aid of God's grace through the intercession of the Holy Helpers.

PRAYER

O GOD, who according to the decrees of Thy providence hast created man for eternal bliss; grant, through the intercession of the Holy

Helpers, that I may attain to my destiny by being united with Thee in this life and loving and praising Thee for ever in heaven. Amen.

Litany and Prayers (p. 88).

THIRD DAY

The Virtue of Faith

Preparatory Prayer (p. 85).

MEDITATION

THE Holy Helpers were so thoroughly imbued with the virtue of divine faith, that they believed its sacred truths with perfect abandonment of their intellect, will, liberty, and whole being. They wavered not amid the severest torments, but remained firm until death in the confession of Christ.

Our time is noted for assaults on the Faith and on the Church that teaches it. The Church, the depository of divine revelation, is blasphemed in her doctrine, in her precepts, in her sacraments, in her ministers, in her cult, in her entire essence. Were you never ashamed of your Catholic name? What cowardliness, what timidity, what downright malice!

PRACTICE

REVIVE your faith by the consideration of the example of the Holy Helpers. Do not, from human respect, neglect the sanctification of the

Lord's Day, the observance of days of fast and abstinence, the reception of the holy sacraments, the profession of your belief in the real presence of Our Lord in the Blessed Sacrament, etc. Meditate frequently on the words of Christ: "He that shall deny Me before men, I will also deny him before My Father who is in heaven"*(*Matt.* x. 33).

Prayer

O GOD, I beseech Thee, through the faith of the Holy Helpers, grant me the grace to treasure in my heart the doctrines of our holy faith, to believe them firmly, to confess them bravely, and to live according to their precepts, that through that same faith I may become worthy to be admitted to Thy beatific vision in heaven. Amen.

Litany and Prayers (p. 88).

FOURTH DAY

The Virtue of Hope

Preparatory Prayer (p. 85).

MEDITATION

"HOPE confoundeth not" (*Rom.* v. 6). According to the commentators these words of Holy Scripture are to be understood in the sense that our works must be in conformity with that which is the object of our hope; that is, we

---

* "Every one therefore that shall confess me before men, I will also confess him before my Father who is in heaven. But he that shall deny me before men, I will also deny him before my Father who is in heaven." (*Matt.* 10:32-33).

must live in such a manner that we really merit the reward of heaven.

We sin against hope also by presumption in God's mercy, by despair, and by over-confidence in our own righteousness. According to Holy Scripture we can not, of our own efficacy, perform a good act, but can do all in Him that strengthens us.

All these truths are exemplified in the lives of the Holy Helpers. Their hope was based on the firm foundation of faith, and consequently, like it, firm, constant, and unwavering.

PRACTICE

LIKE the Holy Helpers, hope to obtain from God all things necessary to salvation, for "the Lord is good to them that hope in Him, to the soul that seeketh Him" (*Lam.* iii. 25). Live so that He can fulfil His promises. Place no obstacle to His bounty and might by a sinful life.

Prayer

ETERNAL God of love and mercy, I thank Thee for all the benefits Thou hast conferred upon me, and hope to obtain, through the intercession of the Holy Helpers, all the graces necessary for my salvation. Through Christ our Lord. Amen.

Litany and Prayers (p. 88).

FIFTH DAY

The Love of God

Preparatory Prayer (p. 85).

MEDITATION

THE love of God which inflamed the Holy Helpers showed forth in their whole life, and particularly at their death. We, too, ought to be inflamed with such love, for without it faith, wisdom, the gift of tongues, and good works in general, avail nothing; for the love of God must inspire them all. "And we know that to them that love God, all things work together unto good" (*Rom.* viii. 28). Such, and such alone, will receive the crown of life. Did not God love us first? To redeem us from sin and eternal death He spared not His only begotten, divine Son. All goods of life and fortune are gifts of His love, evidences of His infinite love. And we find it difficult to return this love? How ungrateful not to love God with your whole heart!

PRACTICE

IMITATE the Holy Helpers in their ardent love of God. Implore their intercession to obtain it. Meditate often on God's love for you, and your heart will be enflamed with love for Him.

Prayer

O GOD of mercy and love, I thank Thee from all my heart for the countless graces which Thy infinite love has bestowed on me. By the ardent love which the Holy Helpers had for Thee, I implore Thee to enkindle in my heart the flame of Thy love, so that I may remain in Thee and Thou in me. Amen.

Litany and Prayers (p. 88).

SIXTH DAY

The Virtue of Charity

Preparatory Prayer (p. 85).

MEDITATION

CHARITY is one of the fundamental virtues of the Christian religion. The moral doctrine preached by Christ is comprised in the words: "Thou shalt love the Lord thy God with thy whole heart, and with thy whole soul, and with thy whole mind. This is the greatest and the first commandment. And the second is like to this. Thou shalt love thy neighbor as thyself. On these two commandments dependeth the whole law and the prophets" (*Matt.* xxii. 37-40).

As in everything else, the Holy Helpers are our exemplars also in charity. Charity consists in wishing well to our fellow-men, rejoicing with the glad and sympathizing with the sad, doing good to all, excusing their faults whenever possible, disclosing them only when necessary, being friendly, indulgent, meek, and helpful toward them. We love our neighbor if we succor the poor and distressed, if we harbor no envy for the rich, if we esteem the just for their virtue, and hate—not the sinner—but sin. We love our neighbor if we are not content with harboring these sentiments in our heart, but show them by our actions.

PRACTICE

ENDEAVOR to exercise this charity according to the spirit of Christ. The love of your neighbor must not be a sentimental affection; it must not originate in casual qualities of character or rank, in inclination, etc., but must have the love of God for its motive. We must exercise charity toward all because God wills it, and in the manner in which He wills it. "Thou shalt love thy neighbor as thyself."

Prayer

O GOD of charity, who dost will that I love my neighbor for Thy sake, grant me the grace, through the intercession of the Holy Helpers, to be animated with that spirit of charity which embraces all and excludes none, which "is patient, kind, envieth not, dealeth not perversely, is not puffed up, is not ambitious, seeketh not her own, is not provoked to anger, thinketh no evil, rejoiceth not in iniquity, but rejoiceth with the truth, beareth all things, believeth all things, endureth all things, and never falleth away" (1 *Cor*. xiii. 4-8). Amen.

Litany and Prayers (p. 88).

SEVENTH DAY

Human Respect

Preparatory Prayer (p. 85).

MEDITATION

BY THE conscientious fulfilment of the duties of their state of life the Holy Helpers show us that the will of God alone was the motive of all their actions. Human respect, regard for the opinion of others, did not influence them.

The cowardly fear, "What will people say?" was the ruin of many a soul. The enemy of mankind is ever intent upon preventing us from doing good through human respect. He insinuates that virtue and piety are out of date and ridiculed. From human respect many a person boasts of that which ought to make him blush; he thinks it discreditable to be less remiss in his religious obligations than others. Ought the opinion and ridicule of the world influence us to prevent our pleasing God? St. Paul says: "If I yet pleased men, I should not be the servant of Christ" (*Gal.* i. 10). Our Lord Himself tells us, "He that shall deny Me before men, I will also deny him before My Father who is in heaven" (*Matt.* x. 33).

PRACTICE

OUR Lord says: "So let your light shine before men, that they may see your good works and glorify your Father who is in heaven" (*Matt.* v. 16). Do not stray from the path of duty on account of human respect; do not let yourself be influenced by the judgments of the world.

Prayer

MERCIFUL God, who gavest the Holy Helpers the grace to fulfil Thy will regardless of human respect; grant that we may obtain through their intercession and merits the courage to despise the opinion of men, and ever serve Thee with a fearless heart. Amen.

Litany and Prayers (p. 88).

EIGHTH DAY

Prayer

Preparatory Prayer (p. 85).

MEDITATION

THE Holy Helpers, well knowing the efficacy of prayer, assiduously devoted themselves to it. From it they drew that wonderful strength which sustained them in their combat for the Faith.

Prayer is the elevation of the mind to God, intercourse with Him by acts of adoration, praise, thanksgiving, and petition. St. Chrysostom says of prayer: "Without prayer it is impossible to lead a good life; for no one can practise virtue except he humbly implores God for it, who alone can give him the necessary strength. Who ceases to love and practise prayer, no longer possesses the gifts of the Spirit. But he that perseveres in the service of God, and deems it an irreparable loss to miss constant prayer, possesses every virtue and is a friend of God."

PRACTICE

OFFER yourself at the beginning of each day to God, and thereby you will belong to Him throughout its whole course. Renew your consecration to Him frequently during the day by short acts of virtue and especially by a good intention, thus rendering all your work a prayer, and you will attain perfection.

Prayer

O GOD, I implore Thee through the merits and intercession of the Holy Helpers, to grant me the spirit of prayer, that following their example I may walk in Thy presence and ever enjoy the

consolation of intercourse with Thee. Through
Christ our Lord. Amen.

Litany and Prayers (p. 88).

NINTH DAY

𝔓erseverance

Preparatory Prayer (p. 85).

MEDITATION

𝔄 VICTORIOUS death was the reward of the
Holy Helpers' perseverance in the service
of God. During this novena you have, no doubt,
formed many good resolutions, exclaiming with
the Royal Prophet, "And I said, now I have begun" (*Ps.* lxxvi. 11). But it happens that many,
despite their good will, become remiss in the pursuit of virtue. Satan is assiduously trying to accomplish their ruin, representing to them and
exaggerating the difficulties to be encountered on
the path of virtue. They hesitate, falter, and finally turn back. This is the most unfortunate
happening that can occur. Of the condition of
such a one Our Lord Himself says: "When the
unclean spirit is gone out of a man, he walketh
through places without water, seeking rest; and
not finding, he saith: 'I will return into my house
whence I came out.' And when he is come, he
findeth it swept and garnished. Then he goeth

and taketh with him seven spirits more wicked than himself, and entering in they dwell there. And the last state of that man becometh worse than the first" (*Luke* xi. 24-26). Are these words not a sufficient warning to encourage us to persevere in our good resolves?

PRACTICE

IN CONCLUDING this novena, survey again the depth of that incomprehensible eternity which is awaiting you. Contemplate in spirit the endless chain of centuries following each other there in reward or in punishment. Does this thought not banish all the difficulties of perseverance?

Prayer

O GOD, whose mercies are infinite and whose goodness is without limit, I beseech Thee through the merits and intercession of the Holy Helpers, grant me the grace of perseverance in Thy love and service to the end. Thou, who dost dispense so many favors through the Holy Helpers, despise not my prayer, but graciously hear and grant it. Amen.

Litany and Prayers (p. 88).

CONCLUDING PRAYER

O FAITHFUL servants of God and powerful protectors of man, Holy Helpers! Since Our Lord appointed you the heavenly advocates for our needs on earth, I confidently turn to you for help in my distress. Countless numbers praise you for aiding them with counsel in doubt, with consolation in anxiety, with health in illness, with safety in danger, with delivery from prison, and with help and assistance in all tribulations. Therefore I, too, have recourse to you, and implore you not to refuse me your aid.

Give thanks to God for me for all the graces He granted me during this novena. I ascribe them to your great merits and powerful intercession. I thank you all together, and each one in particular, for your interest in my favor before the throne of God. I commend myself to your continued protection, that I may one day be united with you in heaven, there to thank the Giver of all good things and to praise Him for all eternity. Amen.

Prayers of Petition and Intercession

Three Invocations

1. GREAT friends of God, Holy Helpers, humbly saluting and venerating you, I implore your help and intercession. Bring my prayers before the throne of the Most Holy Trinity, so that I may experience in all the difficulties and trials of life the mercy of the eternal Father, the love of the incarnate divine Son, and the assistance of the Holy Ghost; that despondency may not depress me when God's wise decree imposes on my shoulders a heavy burden. Above all, I implore your assistance at the hour of death. Help me then to gain the victory over the temptations and assaults of Satan, and to leave this world hopefully trusting in God's mercy, to join you in heaven, there to praise Him for ever and ever. Amen.

2. With confiding trust I turn to you, Holy Helpers, who were selected by God before many other saints to be the special intercessors and advocates of the distressed. Obtain for me strength and courage to struggle and suffer on earth for the glory of God, for the propagation of our holy faith, and for my own perfection. You are fruitful branches of the true and living vine, Jesus Christ, for whom you heroically suffered

Note: Any of these prayers of petition and intercession may be used as a novena—either in combination with the preceding novena prayers, or by itself.

107

hunger and thirst, persecution and ignominy, afflictions and adversity, tortures and death. Here on earth you were true disciples and dauntless martyrs of Christ. Assist me to follow your example and to suffer for His sake, so that I may not be parted from Him as a useless member, but persevere in His service despite all trials and tribulations of life. Knowing my inconstancy and weakness, I have recourse to you, O glorious members of the Church triumphant, and implore you to support my feeble prayers, and to bear them before the throne of the Almighty, who, for your sake, will hear them. Amen.

3. Great friends and servants of God, Holy Helpers! Humbly saluting and venerating you, I implore your help and intercession. God has promised and granted that whosoever invokes your aid shall be relieved in his needs and succored at the hour of death. Therefore I have recourse to you and confidently implore your aid. I am surrounded by difficulties and my soul is oppressed with grief. Burdened with sins, the fear of God's rigorous judgment appalls me, whilst Satan ceases not to exert all his power to accomplish my eternal ruin.

Therefore I implore your assistance, powerful Holy Helpers, in my dire distress. By the penitential life you led, by the cruel tortures you suffered, and by your holy death I entreat you to pray for me. Obtain for me the remission of my sins and perseverance to the end in God's grace. Assist me in my agony and protect me against the wily assaults of Satan, that through your help I may die a happy death and enter a blissful eternity. Amen.

Prayer in Illness

COMPASSIONATE Holy Helpers, who restored health to so many through the power of the name of Jesus; behold me suffering from bodily illness and from wounds of the soul. Implore the kind, merciful Good Samaritan, your and my Lord Jesus Christ, to heal the wounds of my soul by washing them in His most precious blood, and to quicken my spirit by His sanctifying grace. If it, then, be God's holy will and for the welfare of my soul, let me experience the powerful effect of your intercession, that, restored to health, I may serve God with greater fervor, and promote your veneration together with so many who experienced your help in illness and suffering. Amen.

Prayer for the Sick

MERCIFUL Holy Helpers, look benignly upon me, who implore your intercession for a sick person. Our Lord and Redeemer Jesus Christ, who Himself went about healing and doing good, appointed you the special protectors and interces-

sors of the sick, and restored to bodily and spiritual health many for whom you prayed. Encouraged thereby to invoke you, I implore you to offer
up to His sacred Heart all the pains and torments
He suffered during His bitter passion. Offer up
to Him also your own sufferings for God's glory,
which you underwent during life, and in death;
offer up to Him all the anguish and distress suffered by the sick person for whom I invoke your
intercession. Ask Him to restore him to health
of body, and to infuse into his soul the grace
of salvation, so that he may devote his life with
renewed vigor to the service of God and to the
fulfilment of his duties, and thereby gather rich
merits for eternity.

But if God, in the designs of His providence,
should otherwise dispose, implore for the sick
person patience in his illness, resignation to the
divine will, and the grace of a happy death. Assist him in his agony, and conduct his soul to the
throne of the Almighty. Amen.

Prayer of Parents for Their Children

HOLY Helpers, assist me to give thanks to God
for blessing me with children. Having received them from Him, it is my duty to train
them for His service. Therefore I commend
them to your special protection. Guard them
from sin, help them to know and fulfil their

duties, preserve them from all harm of body and soul; pray for them that they may be and remain children of God. For me, obtain the grace always to take good care of them, to edify them by good example, to punish their faults wisely, to preserve their innocence, and to instruct them unto piety, so that they and I may together enjoy the eternal happiness of heaven. Amen.

Prayer of Children for Their Parents

Holy Helpers, mighty intercessors with God in all necessities; God strictly commanded that children should love, honor, and obey their parents. Our Lord and Saviour Jesus Christ Himself gave them the example of submission and obedience by being subject to His mother and foster-father. I commend myself to your powerful intercession and implore you to obtain for me the grace to follow His example. For my parents I implore protection from all evil of body and soul, a long and prosperous life, and a happy death. Reward them for all the care, anxiety, labor, and trouble which they underwent patiently for my sake, with the eternal crown of heavenly glory. Amen.

Prayer of Married People

Holy Helpers, powerful intercessors at the throne of God, by whose providence we were indissolubly joined in holy wedlock through the sacramental bonds of matrimony; obtain for us, through your intercession, the grace to dwell together in mutual love and peace, and to fulfil faithfully the duties of our state of life; that following the example of the saints and elect who lived in wedlock, we may merit God's grace and blessing by a virtuous life here on earth, and united in heaven, praise and bless Him for ever. Amen.

If you have enjoyed this book, consider making your next selection from among the following . . .

Miraculous Images of Our Lady. *Joan Carroll Cruz* 20.00
Eucharistic Miracles. *Joan Carroll Cruz* 13.00
The Four Last Things—Death, Judgment, Hell, Heaven . . 5.00
How to Be Happy, How to Be Holy. *O'Sullivan* 7.00
Little Catechism of the Curé of Ars. *St. John Vianney* . . . 5.50
The Secret of the Rosary. *St. Louis De Montfort* 3.00
Modern Saints—Their Lives & Faces. Bk. 1. *Ball* 18.00
The 12 Steps to Holiness and Salvation. *St. Alphonsus* . . 7.00
Saint Michael and the Angels. *Approved Sources* 5.50
Dolorous Passion of Our Lord. *Anne C. Emmerich* 15.00
Our Lady of Fatima's Peace Plan from Heaven. Booklet. .75
Divine Favors Granted to St. Joseph. *Pere Binet* 4.00
St. Joseph Cafasso—Priest of the Gallows. *St. J. Bosco* . . 3.00
Catechism of the Council of Trent. *McHugh/Callan* 20.00
The Sinner's Guide. *Ven. Louis of Granada* 12.00
Padre Pio—The Stigmatist. *Fr. Charles Carty* 13.50
Why Squander Illness? *Frs. Rumble & Carty* 2.00
The Sacred Heart and the Priesthood. *de la Touche* 7.00
Fatima—The Great Sign. *Francis Johnston* 7.00
Heliotropium—Conformity of Human Will to Divine 11.00
Purgatory Explained. (pocket, unabr.). *Fr. Schouppe* 7.50
Who Is Padre Pio? Radio Replies Press 1.50
The Stigmata and Modern Science. *Fr. Charles Carty* . . . 1.25
The Incorruptibles. *Joan Carroll Cruz* 12.00
The Catholic Religion. *Burbach* 9.00
The Glories of Mary. (pocket, unabr.). *St. Alphonsus* . . . 9.00
Is It a Saint's Name? *Fr. William Dunne* 1.50
Golden Arrow. *Sr. Mary of St. Peter* 10.00
The Holy Shroud & Four Visions. *Fr. O'Connell* 2.00
Clean Love in Courtship. *Fr. Lawrence Lovasik* 2.50
The Prophecies of St. Malachy. *Peter Bander* 5.00
The History of Antichrist. *Rev. P. Huchede* 3.00
Douay-Rheims Bible. Leatherbound 35.00
Where We Got the Bible. *Fr. Henry Graham* 5.00
Imitation of the Sacred Heart of Jesus. *Fr. Arnoudt* 13.50
Baltimore Catechism No. 1. *Kinkead* 3.00
The Way of Divine Love. *Sr. Menendez* 8.50
The Curé D'Ars. *Abbé Francis Trochu* 20.00
Love, Peace and Joy. (St. Gertrude). *Prévot* 5.00

At your Bookdealer or direct from the Publisher.

Prices guaranteed through June 30, 1996.